Star Crossed
Astrology, Personality Theory and the Meeting of Opposites

Also by Clare Martin

Mapping the Psyche Volume 1:
The Planets & the Zodiac Signs

Mapping the Psyche Volume 2:
Planetary Aspects & the Houses of the Horoscope

Mapping the Psyche Volume 3:
Kairos – The Astrology of Time

Alchemy: The Soul of Astrology

Go to www.wessexastrologer.com/authors/Clare-Martin
for Clare's details and links to her video and interviews

Star Crossed
Astrology, Personality Theory and the Meeting of Opposites

Clare Martin

THE WESSEX ASTROLOGER

Published in 2022 by
The Wessex Astrologer Ltd
PO Box 9307
Swanage
BH19 9BF

For a full list of our titles go to www.wessexastrologer.com

© Clare Martin 2022
Clare Martin asserts her moral right to be recognised as
the author of this work

ISBN 9781910531679

Cover design by Andy Jay

A catalogue record for this book is available at The British Library

No part of this book may be reproduced or used in any form or by any means without the written permission of the publisher.
A reviewer may quote brief passages.

Table of Contents

Introduction		vii
Chapter 1	The Psychology of Relationships	1
Chapter 2	The Astrology of Relationships	12
Chapter 3	The Healing Power of Stories	21
Chapter 4	The Cancer/Capricorn Axis The Unwanted Child: Schizoid Adaptation	28
Chapter 5	The Taurus/Scorpio Axis The Abandoned Child: Oral Adaptation	44
Chapter 6	The Gemini/Sagittarius Axis The Owned Child: Symbiotic Adaptation	58
Chapter 7	The Leo/Aquarius Axis The Used Child: Narcissistic Adaptation	73
Chapter 8	The Virgo/Pisces Axis The Defeated Child: Masochistic Adaptation	90
Chapter 9	The Aries/Libra Axis The Exploited Child: Oedipal Adaptation	109
Epilogue	Love Actually	128
Chart Data		135
Bibliography		138
Indexes		142

For one human being to love another: that is perhaps the most difficult of all our tasks, the ultimate, the last test and proof, the work for which all other work is but preparation.

Love is not anything that means merging, giving over, and uniting with another (for what would a union be of something unclarified and unfinished still subordinate?) - it is a high inducement to the individual to ripen, to become something in himself, to become world, to become world for himself for another's sake, it is a great exacting claim upon him, something that chooses him out and calls him to vast things.

Rainer Maria Rilke
Letters to a Young Poet

Introduction

This book explores a question which has been alive for me throughout my astrological and psychotherapeutic career. To what extent can the discoveries of contemporary psychological research be usefully integrated with, and even enhance, astrological practice?

From the earliest times, astrology has interpreted the eternal truths of the human condition as written in the cosmos. It has provided an elegant and inclusive cosmology in which universal and individual patterns are equally reflected. Astrology has an extremely rich historical, philosophical and cultural background. Its categories and forms are archetypal and its language is mythic, symbolic and imaginative.

Current mainstream psychological and psychiatric approaches, on the other hand, emerged out of the medical model originally pioneered by Freud, with its intellectual roots firmly planted in the 'will to science'. The scientific approach is secular, rational, linear and causal, and its language is analytical.[i]

Generally speaking, the focus of contemporary psychotherapy and psychoanalysis is on personal development and growth, well-being, self-actualisation, increased self-reliance, and the achievement of independence and autonomy. This approach generally concerns the development and strengthening of the ego, of consciousness and reason, commitment, responsibility, problem solving, reality testing, controlling and progressing.

---

i James Hillman and Sonu Shamdasani, 'The Lament of the Dead', dialogue between James Hillman, founder of Archetypal Psychology, and Sonu Shamdasani, editor and co-translator of Jung's *Red Book*, and regarded as the leading Jung historian.

Star Crossed: Astrology, Personality Theory and the Meeting of Opposites

Since the end of the 19th century, a vast and powerful new language of psychology has emerged, much of which has been incorporated into mainstream modern thinking and language. It is not unusual these days for people to refer to complexes, neuroses, phobias and personality disorders, such as obsessive compulsion, attention deficit, post-traumatic stress, and any number of other psychological categorisations.

Clinicians who work in private practice and in community mental-health agencies are generally expected to assess client problems within the framework of the fifth edition of the American Psychiatric Association's Diagnostic and Statistical Manual of Mental Disorders (DSM-V) – the 'bible' for making diagnostic assessments. In cases of severe psychopathology, it is used as a guide for medication and other medical treatments.

And yet, both Freud and Jung, the founders of psychoanalysis and analytical psychology respectively, viewed psychopathology mythically, as a valid form of psychological expression, one of the ways the psyche legitimately and spontaneously presents itself.[ii] They believed that each pathology has a valid archetypal perspective, and a mythical approach gives expression to, and validates, the great passions, truths and dramas which reside in the human psyche. Indeed, James Hillman believed that psychopathology is the primary vehicle through which soulfulness is achieved. "Peculiarities are fundamental to soul, as are the hurts, disorders and psychic events which are considered to be abnormal and cannot be altogether repressed, transformed or accepted."[iii] Neither academic psychology nor medical treatment have so far succeeded in eliminating them.

A mythic approach is Dionysian, and mythic figures are "replete with behaviour that, from the secular standpoint, must be classified under criminal pathology, moral monstrosity or personality disorders"[iv].

---

ii James Hillman, (1980) *Facing the Gods*, p2.
iii Ibid, Chapter 1: On the Necessity of Abnormal Psychology.
iv Ibid, *Facing the Gods*, p3.

Introduction

The Greek deities, for example, demonstrate a wide range of what we might now call dysfunctional and even severely pathological behaviours, and madness is a recurring theme. In their dealings with each other and with mankind, the Greek deities could be competitive, jealous, cruel, vengeful and destructive. Shapeshifters, tricksters, murderers, rapists and cannibals, their most heinous crimes, such as incest and murder, were often perpetrated on their own family members. The destructive involvement of the gods in human affairs could affect a family for several generations, and innocent family members would continue to inherit the family curse and suffer accordingly, until it had been finally resolved, redeemed, and the debts to the gods had been paid.

But in our times, these archetypal influences are more likely to be treated purely physiologically, as symptoms to be diagnosed and treated, an observation which caused Jung to comment that 'the gods have become diseases'.[v] As a result, a noticeable rift has grown between the Dionysian, imaginative dimensions of human experience, and the Apollonian, rational, intellectual approach. It is not unusual for the magical or mythic worlds to be viewed with deep suspicion, leading to attempts to control such 'abnormalities' or psychological disturbances.

> "In the absence of archetypal dimensions, man, the measurer of all things, the observer outside, even outside his own suffering, treats it also from outside, observationally, objectively."[vi]

James Hillman believed that the identification of the essential person with 'consciousness' is the faulty heritage of Descartes and nineteenth century psychology. He believed that the language of psychology is *apotropaic*, an attempt to ban the demons or, at the very least, to ban the unknown, as a way of attempting to control and protect ourselves from what lies in the depths of our souls.

---

v C.J. Jung, *Alchemical Studies*, para.54.
vi James Hillman, *Facing the Gods*, p.26.

Star Crossed: Astrology, Personality Theory and the Meeting of Opposites

An analytical approach to psychology or even to the astrological chart involves trying to 'get to the root' of the problem, to solve the puzzle, to uncover the hidden dynamics, to identify the cause and come up with a plausible explanation.

Thomas Moore writes that, according to current notions, a psychologically healthy person is one who has built strong psychic muscles of ego-strength and willpower, and a talent for avoiding pain and risks. "Good mental health is equivalent to sound social and personal adjustment. We expect all normal people to 'keep an even keel, even when the waters are choppy and the winds of spirit reach gale force."[vii]

But the most significant human experiences lie far above or far below the range of normality and stability. The Renaissance scholar and psychological astrologer, Marsilio Ficino, built a theory based on Plato's 'four frenzies', which describe how the awakening of the soul may entail some kind of insanity and instability. He defined poetic madness as access to the imagination, to fantasies, images and symbols, 'a healthy response to a soul filled with discord and dissonance'. Priestly madness occurs when the mind and emotions are given over in worship of the transpersonal mysteries. Prophetic madness requires a separation of the soul from the body in which the categories of time are no longer limiting and it becomes possible to see things from the perspective of timelessness. Erotic madness, or love, may be painfully exhilarating and disastrously pleasant, but above all it is necessary for the soul. Thomas Moore writes that anyone who has loved knows that it is a madness, and the core of Ficino's psychology of love consists in the capacity of human love to entice the soul away from the multiple attractions of materialism towards the pleasures of soul-values.

The question, therefore, is whether astrology, as psychology's much older sister, needs to be carefully protected from the materialistic reductionism of modern psychological thinking. Or is there is a way in

---

[vii] Thomas Moore, (1990), *The Planets Within: The Astrological Psychology of Marsilio Ficino*, Lindisfarne Books, revised edition.

which these two very different approaches to the human condition can be usefully and creatively integrated? The following chapters explore this question, and present some of the remarkable similarities and some of the differences between personality theories and psychological astrology.

Chapter 1

The Psychology of Relationships

Contemporary Character Analysis

Developmental Psychology, Personality Theory[i], Object Relations Theory, Ego and Self Psychology, Relational Psychoanalysis, Attachment Theory and Transactional Analysis are all *systems theories* which seek to describe the psychological structures we build in order to function in the world. They study the ways we express our personality *in terms of behaviour*. Their common focus is the study of the natural evolution of ego development and the effects of distress and inner conflict on ego functioning. Ongoing empirical and clinical research has led to an emerging and generally recognised synthesis of approaches, known generically as 'Contemporary Character Analysis'.

Systems theorists recognise that human beings develop and exist in a dual world and therefore always within a context of relationship, caught between subject and object, self and other, internal and external, at both conscious and unconscious levels. Practitioners in these fields believe that it is the way we interpret and internalise our first experiences of the outside world which sets the scene for our personality development, the psychological structures we build and the mechanisms we use in order to function in the world. In other words, experiences in our early infancy continue to exert a strong influence throughout our adult lives.

---

i   Stephen M Johnson, *The Symbiotic Character* (1980), *Characterological Transformation: The Hard Work Miracle* (1985), *Humanizing the Narcissistic Style* (1987), *Character Styles* (1994).

Systems theories have been arrived at empirically. They emerged from decades of dedicated clinical research and practice initially carried out by psychologists and psychoanalysts[ii] during the late nineteenth and twentieth centuries.

Although they are essentially a development of Freudian psychoanalytic theory, systems theorists and practitioners believe that the instinctual needs of the developing child go well beyond the internal oral, anal and phallic pressures posited by Freud. Rather than seeing the human being as a system of biological drives, they place *relationship* at the heart of human development.

The five stages of Character Development

Systems theorists have identified five stages of character development.[iii] The first stage is *self-affirmation* – the infant's initial expression of its life force and instinctual needs.

During the first 18 months of life, the newly born infant is barely other than 'one with the universe'. If a child's physical and emotional needs are recognised, sufficiently accommodated and affirmed at each stage of his development, he will thrive both physically and emotionally, learn to think clearly, gradually gain confidence and self-agency, and learn to take proper care of himself and of others.

But in the second stage, and to a greater or lesser extent, the initial expression of the infant's instinctual needs will inevitably be frustrated or meet with a ***negative response*** from his environment or from his carers. His existence may be met with hostility or coldness and his basic needs repeatedly denied or ignored. Because this initial rejection occurs at a

---

ii Significant contributors to this field are: Kurt Lewin (1890-1947), Ronald Fairbairn (1889 – 1964), D.W. Winnicott (1896-1971), Margaret Mahler (1897-1985), Harry Guntrip (1901–75) Edward John Bowlby (1907-90) Eric Burne (1910-70), Heinz Kohut (1913-81), Daniel Stern (1934–2012).

iii Stephen Johnson: *Character Styles*.

pre-verbal stage of development, before the infant is capable of any kind of abstract thinking or rationalisation, it is internalised in the form of undifferentiated global statements about himself and about the world. Is the world sufficiently safe, resilient and nurturing, or is it uncertain, painful and precarious? It is these primal perceptions which profoundly shape the infant's capacity to trust.

In the third stage, the infant reacts to the frustration or negation of his instinctive life force with ***rage, terror*** and/or ***grief***. At this stage, provided that the parental response is modified, the normal healthy development of the infant can still proceed. But if it is not modified, then the infant is forced to turn against himself. No infant can withstand exclusion from parental approval and protection, and so he learns to curb his natural impulses. The rejected, denied and suppressed instincts are consigned to the unconscious, from whence they continue to operate autonomously.

It is in the two final stages that character is formed. The fourth stage is ***self-negation.*** The child feels guilty and turns against himself by identifying with the negative parental or social environment. This is the beginning of an internal conflict which can persist throughout a lifetime. The infant suppresses his own life force, stifles his autonomy, denies his need for support and holds back his love. Energetically oriented therapists, such as Wilhelm Reich believed that the blocks to self-expression are literally present in the body, causing chronic muscular tension which is very resistant to change. The body blocks are attempts to avoid the anxiety of being vulnerable again and risking the anticipated re-injury.

The fifth stage is the ***adjustment process***, which involves the construction of a 'provisional personality', 'false self', or 'ego ideal' all of which are compromises designed to make the best of the situation. The infant attempts to 'rise above' his natural self and live up to an 'ideal' by developing a set of attitudes, behaviours and strategies which he believes will gain the acceptance he craves and which, at the very least, will ensure his survival. In order to make sense of his experiences, he constructs an internal world which corresponds to his early external reality.

The provisional personality, false self or ego ideal are defence mechanisms, constructed in an attempt to create safety, cohesion and consistency. Defence structures are designed to protect the mysterious inner core of the personality from intolerable internal and/or external threats. Given the infant's limited equipment and limited experience of the world, these early adaptations, or compromises, enable a functional adaptation to the real world. But they continue to affect us deeply for the rest of our lives, which explains why our behaviour in subsequent relationships is often 'childish' and 'irrational', since it harks back to the very young and frightened child who made a partial and primitive adaptation to a hostile environment.

Character Structures

Character structures or personality styles can be defined as a set of attitudes, behaviours and strategies developed in response to our earliest experiences of the world and of other people. These adaptations are constructed in order to gain recognition, acceptance and validation in the eyes of others. They equate psychologically to the development of the *ego*.

It is the parts of the real self which we exaggerate and the parts we suppress which define our character and which eventually become recognisable as our **Character or Personality Style.** Each personality adaptation has its own rewards, and is responsible for many of our greatest skills and achievements. As we develop psychologically, these structures become ever more sophisticated, complex and intricate.

The *ego* can be understood as the construction of a personality we choose to identify with, how we wish to see ourselves and how we wish others to see us. It is a normal and necessary adaptation and, once we have settled for our 'ego ideal' there is an understandable resistance to its extinction. But over-identification with the *ego* can become increasingly restrictive, one-sided and suffocating as we grow, mature and develop psychologically. Eventually, it can effectively isolate parts of ourselves from other parts, and/or from more realistic interactions with others. The more threatening an infant's intra-psychic or inter-personal reality is, the more extreme, rigid, inflexible and entrenched our character or personality styles tend to become over time.

Behind the *ego* lurks what Jung referred to as the *shadow*: the repressed parts of us which we come to believe are unacceptable or evil, and therefore try to hide from ourselves and others, usually by rendering them unconscious. But the *shadow* also contains aspects of our wholeness, innate potential, longings and creative energy which have not been recognised or welcomed in the environment into which we are born.

Since we each possess an *ego* and a conflicting unconscious *shadow*, this means that we all have, to a greater or lesser extent, split personalities. The psychotherapeutic task is to become conscious of this split and to find a way of reconciling the inner opposites, so as to create, or recreate, a more flexible, balanced, and unified sense of ourselves.

All character adaptations are solutions to old problems, based on the resources available at the time of their construction. For adults, they have usually outlived their usefulness and are now far more trouble than they are worth, but they persist.

No matter how successfully adapted or well-adjusted we become, each personality style is a defence mechanism, originally constructed to protect us from re-experiencing the anxiety and tension of an original problem or trauma. Personality styles continue to be reinforced and become self-perpetuating unless, and until, we are able to see that they have something to do with us. An understanding of our own major character adaptations can help us recognise the 'repetition compulsions' which keep us on the same problematic treadmills. It is only when we can recognise the parts we ourselves are playing in the story that we begin to have choices.

Star Crossed: Astrology, Personality Theory and the Meeting of Opposites

Character structures limit us to the extent that they become rigidly defended, but can be the source of animation, renewal and authenticity as they become more flexible. Transformation happens through our character structures, not in spite of them. Our potential for wholeness and self acceptance lies *within* and *beneath* the character defences we have built for ourselves. Each of the character structures revolves around a specific problem or challenge, and there are many well-known stories, myths and films which explore, illustrate and expand on these themes. Recognising our own stories within them can have a remarkably therapeutic effect, leading to increased insight, self-acceptance and psychological integration.

Astrology and Personality Theory

What is particularly interesting is that the character styles we adopt appear to be not only universal but also limited in number.

Character styles describe patterns of human adaptation and behaviour which appear to describe very accurately, and deepen our understanding of, the tension of the many dualities and polarities in the natal chart. As such, they describe patterns of human encounter and exchange which provide valuable clues to the interpretation of relationship patterns embedded in the birth chart.

It is here that astrological and psychological approaches can find common ground. A knowledge of personality theory can enhance, enrich and deepen our understanding of the dynamic relationship themes which exist on the astrological axes, and, as such, can be usefully integrated into astrological practice.

Different systems theorists use a variety of different assessment criteria, but there are usually between six and eight main **character styles,** or patterns of behaviour, each of which describes a fundamental inner conflict, and each of which exists on a spectrum with two opposite poles. Stephen Johnson has identified six main character styles, which appear to describe with remarkable accuracy the inherent tension of the six astrological axes.

The following chapters explore the relationship between **character styles** and the **astrological axes**. They are presented in the order of the developmental periods in which particular instinctual needs are believed to arise. These stages describe the developing infant's need to attach or bond to a primary caregiver, to individuate through exploration, self-determined activity and self-expression, and the building of healthy psychic boundaries and attuned self-other relationships.

The **Cancer/Capricorn** and **Taurus/Scorpio** character styles share primal attachment and bonding as their central developmental issue, typically believed to be forged pre-natally and during the first nine months of life.

The **Gemini/Sagittarius, Leo/Aquarius** and **Virgo/Pisces** character styles originate from the initial period of self-development, which occurs between the ages of one and three. With a good enough fit between the infant, his environment and his carers, the child will feel sufficiently supported and safe enough to explore and learn on his own, gradually growing in self-confidence and developing the capacity for self-reflection.

The **Aries/Libra** character style is initially forged between the ages of three and five, when the child begins to recognise his own place in the wider world, primarily in the family system, and subsequently in the educational and social systems.

The table below lists each major stage of natural child development, and the expected emotional reaction if any of these stages is blocked or thwarted. In such cases, the child internalises his experiences of the world in terms of his **wounded self**. The resulting character styles are descriptive and not necessarily pathological. It all depends on the level of disturbance experienced.

Johnson identifies three levels of adaptation for each character structure. In *normal character styles*, there will be an awareness of, and relatively successful navigation of the stress of inner conflict. At the *neurotic* level, the internal conflict will be experienced as long standing, life-disrupting and self-defeating. At the *personality disorder* level, there will be a low level of ego strength, the inability to contain a variety of affective states and a marked disruption in functioning.

Personality Theory: Structural Character Development
[Stephen M. Johnson: Character Styles]

Axis	Developmental Issue	Emotional Reaction if Thwarted	Internalisation - The Wounded Self	Resulting Character Style
Cancer/ Capricorn	Safety	Terror	The Hated Child	Schizoid
Taurus/ Scorpio	Need	Voracious rage	The Abandoned Child	Oral
Gemini/ Sagittarius	Self-Agency	Panic	The Owned Child	Symbiotic
Leo/Aquarius	Self Esteem	Impotent Fury	The Used Child	Narcissistic
Virgo/Pisces	Self-Determination	Defiant Anger	The Defeated Child	Masochistic
Aries/Libra	Self-Expression	Deep Hurt	The Exploited Child	Oedipal

Personality theory recognises that, although each person may have a predominant character style, a mixture of structural functioning will apply to any given person, with at least three character styles usually being significant. The same is true with the horoscope, since every birth chart contains all six of the astrological axes, at least three of which are likely to have particular emphasis.

Our experience of reality is complex and multi-levelled and the natal chart tells us that we live simultaneously in multiple realities. But astrologers can identify which of the axes are particularly emphasized and therefore which of the character styles are most likely to be constellated. This is very simple astrology, but can be extremely helpful and useful in chart interpretation.

Occasionally, of course, the planets will be spread more or less evenly throughout a birth chart, with none of the axes being particularly emphasized. People with splash pattern charts, for example, tend to have many interests in many different areas of life, but can also scatter their energies. In extreme cases this can lead to a deeply disturbed sense of identity, or radical dissociation, resulting in exceptionally unstable, impulsive, reckless or volatile behaviour, recognised in the DSMV as *multiple personality disorder*, now normally referred to as *dissociative identity disorder*, or *borderline personality disorder*. Developmental psychologists recognise that dissociation is usually an attempt to survive complex trauma during childhood, such as physical, emotional and sexual abuse or severe neglect, at a time when the brain and personality are developing. But, even if our environment is no longer traumatic, it can continue as an outgrown defensive adaptation which protects us from having to process past trauma.

Transpersonal approaches such as *psychosynthesis*[iv], expand the boundaries by identifying a deeper centre of identity, a unifying or central principle of consciousness, known as the core Self. The Self can be described as the conductor of the orchestra, analogous to the dot in the centre of the birth chart, capable of synthesizing the many different aspects of our character into a greater whole.

Psychopathology

In their more extreme and dysfunctional forms, character structures are widely used for psychiatric diagnoses. Personality disorders and even full-blown pathological conditions are believed to occur when any particular

---

iv see Roberto Assagioli, *Psychosynthesis* (1965), *Jung and Psychosynthesis* (1967), *The Act of Will* (1973)].

polarity becomes radically split or dissociated, and therefore no longer capable of self-balancing.

Like a pendulum, the more we identify consciously with one pole on any axis, the more extreme the opposite, unconscious, pole becomes, until it appears to function autonomously, as a complex, or shadow quality, outside our conscious will. When any axis becomes temporarily or permanently broken or severed, the ego is flooded and overwhelmed by the collective content of the unconscious. Jung believed that a complex only becomes pathological when we assume that we do not have it – because then it has us. "In this sense potential psychopathology is an integral part of our human structure."[v] It all depends how polarised each axis becomes.

For example, the two core fears of **abandonment** and **engulfment** are believed to describe the universal double bind recognised by child development psychologists. On the one hand, we are all terrified of abandonment, since we were initially completely dependent on the other for our survival, and on the other hand, we are equally afraid of engulfment, since we must develop self-agency and sufficient self-confidence if we are to learn to stand on our own feet, to thrive and develop in the world.

These core fears are normal and generally navigable, and it is usual to be on both sides of the dynamic at different times, but the point is that they relate to the past. As rational, mature adults, we know that we can take care of ourselves and make our own decisions, but our underlying fears hark back to the terrifying primal experience of being completely dependent and defenceless.

If these core fears become extreme, they become extreme together, with one fear predominating consciously, and the other just as powerfully influencing us from the unconscious. In other words, the level of our conscious fear of abandonment is directly proportional to the level of our unconscious fear of engulfment, and vice versa.

---

v Edward Whitmont, *The Symbolic Quest*, p.167.

Character styles describe recognisable patterns of human encounter and exchange which provide valuable clues to the interpretation of relationship patterns embedded in the birth chart. Working mythically, astrologers can usefully explore and discuss with their clients the archetypal relationship themes which may well be finding expression in their lives.

The description of the character styles outlined above is necessarily over-simplistic, since a thorough and detailed study of clinical, therapeutic and psychiatric diagnoses and treatment is not only beyond the scope of this book, but also generally beyond the scope of astrological practice. Nevertheless, at the level of what Stephen Johnson refers to as *normal character styles,* I believe that they can be usefully integrated into the work of psychologically oriented astrologers.

Chapter 2

The Astrology of Relationships

Plato's *Symposium* is a philosophical text dated c.385-370, describing a friendly contest of speeches given by a group of notable Athenians during a banquet. The speeches are to be given in praise of Eros, the god of love and desire.

When the time comes for the comic playwright Aristophanes to speak, he describes how, long ago, there were three types of human beings, male, female and androgynous. But they were highly ambitious and their strength and power were terrifying, so Zeus and the rest of the gods met in council to decide what to do with them. They resolved not to destroy them, since that would mean the gods would no longer receive their worship and sacrifices.

Eventually it was decided to split every human being into two halves. The wound of separation would make them weaker and ensure they behaved more moderately in the future. But when this was done, each half longed so much for their other half that they began to die of starvation and general apathy. For Aristophanes, love and desire are the 'pursuit of wholeness', the recovery of our original nature. The human race will flourish when people find their other halves, their hearts' desire.

Like Aristophanes' original human beings, the natal chart describes our wholeness. It contains everything we need to know about our relationship with ourselves, the world and other people. And yet, it also describes how we have become split into two, since every natal chart reveals a series of fundamental polarities, between opposing signs, houses, angles, planets and nodes. Each half longs for the other, for the recovery of our original wholeness.

The Law of Opposites

Dane Rudhyar writes that "reality has a rhythmic heart".[i] We are all subject to the ancient concept of the waxing and waning of the two universal forces, the yin and the yang, the ebb and flow of life, the breathing in and breathing out. In other words, the waning of energy of one pole within any system is always associated with the waxing in strength of the opposite pole.

These opposing principles constantly challenge each other, separating and reuniting and ultimately balancing each other. To the extent that we succeed in finding a balance within, the two polarities of human experience can be expressed in dynamic harmony "our lives will become a true expression of the underlying pulse of life within which we exist."[ii]

Working with the many polarities in the horoscope, the house and sign axes, the angles and planetary oppositions, astrologers know how difficult it is to accept, let alone integrate, both ends of any axis. The opposition is an aspect of maximum tension, with each pole on a spectrum appearing to be mutually exclusive, leading to feelings of paralysis, of literally being caught between two poles. But it is out of this tension that awareness is born, which ensures that neither pole becomes either too extreme or autonomous. It is the drama of being caught between opposites, the internal conflicts which are constellated in our dealings with the world and with other people, which makes life so interesting and, ultimately, creative.

All axes are self-balancing systems and, if we can consciously hold the tension of opposing signs, houses, angles and planets, which is always an uncomfortable and difficult thing to do, this can lead to important insights, greater understanding and self-knowledge, modesty, increased humour and self-acceptance, and more compassion for ourselves and others.

But, in order to avoid the anxiety generated by the tension of opposing forces and values, we generally find it much easier to identify with one end

---
i   Dane Rudhyar, (1978) *The Pulse of Life*, Chapter 1, p.11.
ii Ibid.

of each spectrum – the one which is most in line with our ego, or conscious values - and to deny, reject, or project the other. The rejected pole falls into the unconscious, from where it acts as a beacon, exerting an even more powerful influence. Our shadow qualities reside in the disowned end of the spectrum, and are then constellated in our relationships, through which we meet the unconscious contents of our own psyches.

Astrology tells us that it is the *nature* we are born with which defines our reality. The relationship themes described in the birth chart are real to us, regardless of the actual reality of other people or of the outside world. In other words, we don't really see anyone else at all, insofar as they are independent of our projections upon them. Everyone we meet simply tells us more about ourselves, which is why relationships cannot be looked at 'objectively'. Neither the problem nor the solution resides in 'the other' and, if we are working psychologically, we know that our relationship problems will not be solved once the right partner is found, since all our relationships will be reflections of the quality of the relationship we have with ourselves.

Rather, we find ourselves attracted to people who, and situations which, enable us to repeat and reinforce our own personal stories. Relationships are usually formed when there is a mutual astrological resonance, and it is this which provides the 'glue' between two people.

The law of resonance[iii] states that, in order to perceive something, a person needs a corresponding vibration in themselves. It is this resonance, like a radio frequency, which makes perception possible. Like the extreme ends of the light and sound spectrums, anything which lies outside our capacity to resonate cannot be perceived by us, and therefore does not exist for us. And this explains why relationships can only be formed with people with whom we share a resonance. People who don't resonate with our story are boring – there is no new material, nothing to be learned - and people who do are exciting – there is something to be explored. This resonance

---

iii See Thorwald Dethlefsen, (1984) *The Challenge of Fate*.

can either be sympathetic – an affinity or attraction – or antipathetic – an aversion or repulsion – but, either way, it tells us something about ourselves. Our environment and other people are mirrors, reflecting back to us what we cannot see without their help.

Once a relationship is formed, we almost always, although unknowingly, go about attempting to turn the 'other' into our preconceived expectations, and to 'draw out' certain responses and reactions from them. And at the same time, the people in our lives will, however unconsciously, be attempting to repeat and reinforce their own preconceived expectations and personal stories, by provoking certain responses from us.

All relationships polarise, and the extreme ends of any polarity both repel and attract each other in equal measure. The roles we play can switch suddenly from one end of a spectrum to the other. Human nature being what it is, when we identify with one sign, house or planet, the opposite sign, house or planet must always be taken into consideration, since it is just as, or even more, important. For example, the sign of Libra includes Aries, the sign of Aquarius includes Leo, the second house must include the eighth house, the twelfth house must include the sixth house, and so on. As Dane Rudhyar wrote, "it simply does not make any sense to try and define the meaning of one end of an axis without including in the definition the meaning of the other end."[iv]

Ultimately, from a developmental point of view, the psychological purpose of relationships seems to be the re-constellation, reinforcement and continued perpetuation of our very early experiences. Recognising the major character styles in our charts, and the repetition compulsion which keeps us on the same old treadmills, we can come to realise that, in our adult relationships, we are making an unconscious attempt to relive, rework and resolve past conflicts or losses, and that we can even outgrow a story when the need is met.

---

iv Dane Rudhyar, *The Astrological Houses*, p.154.

Star Crossed: Astrology, Personality Theory and the Meeting of Opposites

From an astrological point of view, it is our relationship joys and struggles, be they with partners, parents, siblings, bosses, co-workers, friends, and so on, which provide us with the most valuable information about our original wholeness, and how we are seeking, eventually, to come home to ourselves.

Becoming more conscious of our inner opposites not only generates psychic development, but can be a great relief, as we come to realise that what appear to be mutually exclusive polarities are in fact not only equally true but dependent upon one another. True self-acceptance has a kind of musical quality. It is the ability to dance between the opposite poles of each spectrum of experience. We no longer have to hold rigidly to one 'socially acceptable' view of ourselves, the ego-approved view, but can come to accept and include the previously projected or denied parts of ourselves, our gifts, talents and potential, our joys and fears, foibles and failures, our inadequacies and neuroses, as belonging to the same spectrum of experience. In doing so, we can come to accept and celebrate ourselves, other people and the world just as they are, with all their apparent contradictions.

Astrologers can never tell from the chart itself exactly where, on any particular spectrum, a person will be consciously identified. But we do know that, when we are consciously identified with one pole of an axis, then the opposite, balancing pole will be just as important.

An appreciation of the inherent tension which exists on each axis brings us closer to understanding the psychological dynamic which drives each polarity. As we become more familiar with this way of thinking and interpreting the chart, it becomes ever easier to recognise these patterns in ourselves and others. And this, I believe, is where a knowledge of personality theory and character styles can be so helpful. The table below describes the polarities inherent within each sign axis.

The Relational Birth Chart

SIGNS	RULING PLANETS	NATURAL HOUSES	PSYCHOLOGICAL DYNAMIC
Cancer/ Capricorn	Moon/ Saturn	4th/10th	**Axis of Incarnation** Child/Parent Home/World Private Life/Public Life Belonging/Supporting The Tribe/The Hermit
Taurus/ Scorpio	Venus/Mars (Pluto)	2nd/8th	Axis of Exchange Mine/Yours Valuing Self/Other Dependency on Self/Other Retention/Release Incorporation/Elimination
Gemini/ Sagittarius	Mercury/ Jupiter	3rd/9th	**Axis of Exploration** Learning/Teaching Information/Meaning Intellect/Beliefs Student/Teacher Near/Far
Leo/ Aquarius	Sun/Saturn (Uranus)	5th/11th	**Axis of Identity** Self/Society The Individual/The Collective The Heart/The Head Personal Good/Common Good Autocracy/Democracy Egocentrism/Altruism
Virgo/Pisces	Mercury/ Jupiter (Neptune)	6th/12th	**Axis of Service** Order/Chaos Control/Trust Duty/Compassion Self-sufficiency/Co-dependency Form/Content
Aries/Libra	Mars/Venus	1st/7th	**Axis of Equilibrium** Self/Not Self, Me/You Competition/Accommodation Autonomy/Compromise Self Agency/Co-operation

Star Crossed: Astrology, Personality Theory and the Meeting of Opposites

Birth charts contain every polarity in the above table, but to a greater or lesser extent, depending on the individual chart. Every birth chart reveals a range of distinct themes, each with its own strengths and challenges, but there are usually at least three axes which are particularly emphasized in any birth chart.

Astrologers are in the unique position of being able to identify from the birth chart which of the axes are particularly relevant and therefore which of the polarities, or life stories, are most likely to be constellated. This is very simple astrology, but extremely useful and practical.

The **ASC/DES** is perhaps the most important axis of all, since it represents the potential for an equal balance of power in one-to-one adult relationships. At birth our personal survival (Ascendant) is literally dependent on 'the other', on our parents or carers (Descendant) and, as we begin to adapt to outside influences, we develop a very early and heightened sensitivity to the reactions and attitudes of others towards us. Our first experience of ourselves is therefore derived from the way we are 'mirrored' by others.

But it is on this axis that we build a sense of ourselves as individuals, not in isolation but through our relationships with significant others. The planets in the 7th house, and the sign on the Descendant, through its planetary ruler/s, almost always describe qualities which belong to us but which we project onto others.

The MC/IC axis and its planetary rulers are always important, since it reflects the tension and creativity of the meeting of opposites which resulted in our conception. We inherit and absorb the parental dynamic, the parental atmosphere, which is generated not only by their outward behaviour, but even more powerfully by the underlying emotions between them. Parental conflicts, such as unexpressed resentment or hostility, conscious or unconscious, are experienced by the child as if they were his own, and he reacts to conflict tension with guilt. The parents' relationship profoundly affects our capacity for trust and intimacy, and sets the pattern for all subsequent relationships.

No matter how harmonious, happy, polarised or dysfunctional the parental relationship is or was, it is deeply embedded within our psyches as our relationship blueprint and remains a powerful influence for our entire lives. To the extent that we remain emotionally enmeshed in our family patterns, and often in spite of our best intentions, we will continue to repeat the very same themes in our adult relationships with what seems like uncanny predictability. There is always a powerful, insistent and often extremely creative ancestral 'charge' around this axis, and it is here that we seem to inherit the as yet unfulfilled, incomplete, still to be manifested or resolved, destiny and calling of our family line.

Other particularly significant relationship themes are found on the axis containing the Sun, the all-important nodal axis, as well as any axis containing a stellium or powerful set of planetary oppositions.

But although the birth chart itself remains the same throughout our lives, it cannot, of course, be explained by, or reduced to, a set of clinical or diagnostic categories. It is also a dynamic energy system, and real and profound change is possible. Transits, directions and progressions continue to unfold and to reflect the moving kaleidoscope of our natal patterns. As our experience and insight deepens and we come to know ourselves better, we can learn to integrate our inner opposites and live more consciously and creatively, which is the common goal of both personality theory and psychological astrology.

Working psychologically, the astrological focus is not so much on the cards we have been dealt at birth, but on what we do with them, how we play our hand. It is never possible for an astrologer to know, in advance, how an individual will experience and engage with their own natal chart. Each of the six sign and house axes describes what appears to be an impossible double-bind, reflecting an archetypal theme and telling a story which is both universal and uniquely personal, each one of which carries the potential for creative resolution. It is remarkable, and even awe-inspiring, to witness how often people master and resolve what appear to be extremely painful, harsh or challenging natal configurations.

Chapter 3

The Healing Power of Stories

In traditional cultures, bards, storytellers, poets, healers and shamans knew that the deities and nature spirits were the powers that determined fate, sometimes acting on behalf of individuals and cultures and at other times creating strife and conflict. Mysterious disturbances, such as visions, dreams and altered states of consciousness were, once upon a time, understood as communications from the other worlds. Throughout history, storytellers have carried the cultural myths from generation to generation, providing individuals, and even whole cultures, with mythic and imaginative contexts which have provided orientation, guidance and ways of navigating human experience.

Myths, legends and stories transcend time – they are narrative patterns that give meaning and significance to our lives - a way of making sense of our world. The core themes which lie at the root of all great literature describe the truth of the human condition. As such, they never pass judgement or tell us what we should or shouldn't do, but tell us instead what will happen in a particular set of circumstances.

The psychoanalyst Rollo May[i] believed that contemporary therapy is almost entirely concerned with the problems of the individual's search for myths. In his view, the loss of our cultural myths was the main reason for the birth and development of psychoanalysis in the first place. He believed that the repression or denial of the myths alive within us can eventually lead to the partial, periodic or even total overwhelming of a person's conscious mind. Myths and stories, whether read, spoken, listened to or

---
[i] Rollo May, *The Cry for Myth*.

watched, awaken the imagination and feed the soul, and a nourished soul gains a sense of meaning, perspective and coherence.

Our culture has lost its mythic moorings, and therefore lacks the soul nourishment it needs. Dismissed by defensive ego-consciousness, the hidden pressures continue to build until a range of psychological or physical symptoms emerge. Many of the problems of society in our day, such as the increase in addictions of all kinds, depression and even suicide, can be traced back to the lack of core, collective myths. Jung believed that neuroses are the consequence of the suffering of a soul which has not discovered its meaning. As he famously wrote, "The foundation of all mental illness is the unwillingness to experience legitimate suffering".[ii]

We are now challenged to do for ourselves what in previous ages was done by family, custom, church and state. Our task, if we wish to remain sane, is to bring some order and coherence into our consciousness, either from within or without.

Great stories teach us that life and human relationships are complex and multidimensional, paradoxical, often tortured, and ever-evolving. Discovering the archetypal landscape of each character structure can encourage us to embrace paradox and develop a dialogue between our own inner opposites. Through story, we can develop the ability to hold our experience of reality lightly and flexibly.

And this is where astrology can help. Birth charts are life stories, and every planet has an essential myth or story at its core. Charts have patterns – incidents of the same or similar type keep reoccurring. People find themselves in the same kind of situations and continue to experience similar outcomes in their relationships, careers or finances. Finding the stories brings a chart to life – gives it energy, depth and direction. As the planets come alive and begin to express their essential meanings, so we can anticipate how they will react in particular situations. And that means

---

ii C.G. Jung, (CW18) *The Symbolic Life*, para 1578.

that, once we have discovered the myths within, we can seek to be true to the essential and always paradoxical energy in our birth charts.

In a chart reading it makes all the difference if an experience that someone is going through is placed in a mythic, imaginative or poetic context. This transforms the experience from what might feel like a petty, personal mess to be ashamed of, into a recognisable archetypal human pattern, or dilemma. This restores our dignity, and removes the temptation to judge ourselves or others.

Presented as a drama within a particular historical and cultural context, the strength of a story depends on its ability to touch on universally significant human experiences, enduring themes and patterns which transcend culture and time, which are yet wrapped inside a unique, personal set of circumstances. Stories are mirrors in which we can see our own reflection. They help us to see our own personal struggles and conflicts as universal aspects of human experience. They open the imagination and provide us with a language with which to communicate the truths which reside within our souls.

Stories begin with a situation which lacks wholeness; where there is no conflict there is no story. The conflict can be between characters, within a character, or both. In external conflict, characters struggle against the environment or with each other. In internal conflict, the characters struggle with their own opposing motivations, values or choices. Often there is more than one conflict, each of which constitutes a kind of sub-plot within the overall story structure. This is what creates suspense, and in the unfolding drama, the main characters either resolve the conflicts or do not. Many stories describe a rite of passage, or some lesson that the main characters have to learn.

Stories which stand the test of time adhere to the well-established rules of storytelling. Once we recognise the general pattern or theme of the story, we know roughly how it will unfold, including a range of potential outcomes. At that point, we can decide whether or not to engage with it and, if it holds our attention, allow ourselves to become emotionally involved.

Entering fully into a story requires a kind of surrender, as we cross the threshold from the literal world into the world of the imagination, where we can engage with a vast range of emotions. The stories we are drawn to – either by attraction or repulsion – tell us more about ourselves. Stories which do not engage us or draw us in, or which we find boring, are not relevant to our souls.

Sometimes we need to hear a story, read a book or watch a film many times, until its deeper meanings have been fully explored, and the emotions associated with them have all been used up. When we understand our stories we can make better choices, and even outgrow a story when a need is met.

Storytellers are meaning-makers, and in this sense, astrologers have an important therapeutic function. Like skilled weavers, astrologers can gather together all the disparate threads in a birth chart, and combine them into a richly textured, archetypally coherent tapestry.

Astrologers can find the stories which bring a birth chart to life, exploring natal themes from a mythic perspective, touching on themes which ring eternally true, through history and across cultures. Such stories direct attention away from analytical assessment, clinical diagnosis and treatment, and extend the bandwidth of what is normal, embracing the oddities and peculiarities of the human condition, with all its paradoxes, complexities and pathologies.

Understanding our stories is empowering, as we gain increased insight and self-knowledge. We begin to see our patterns more clearly, and recognise in ourselves the temptation, or even compulsion, to go on repeating them. We can use this knowledge as a path which leads towards progressive development and integration. Each experience modifies awareness, and every new episode has the potential to alter consciousness as we learn, develop insight and realise our potentials over time.

Contemporary mainstream psychology developed as an empirical science, concerned with discrimination and categorisation, based on case-study work and statistical analyses. But it is equally valid to approach an understanding of human nature through the arts, including literature, drama and poetry. Such an approach is not designed to assess, or judge what is 'normal' or 'abnormal', and not concerned with diagnosis or treatment. It is led by a fascination with human nature, just as it is, with all its peculiarities and perversions, kindnesses and cruelty, humour and suffering. Stories are descriptive amplifications of human behaviour, and are filled with rich material which does not exclude paradox, hypocrisy, deception, cruelty, blindness or any other so-called human abnormalities.

Once the characters in a story come to life, then all kinds of emotional activity emerges; the human passions and motivations, the loves and hates, joys and tragedies. In the end, it is our inadequacies and weaknesses, our neediness and vulnerability, our tragedies and crises which describe the whole human picture.

The Healing Power of Films

Film makers and directors have become the modern storytellers and meaning makers, and films are increasingly recognised as a serious psychological medium.[iii]

The great film directors capture the psychological energy of the archetypes at work in our lives, continually reworking and dressing them in different clothes. The dark mystery and hidden power of Pluto, the god of the underworld, for example, has been recast as Darth Vader in the Star Wars films, or Voldemort in the Harry Potter films. The shadow side of Neptune has been recast as the Nazgul, or Ringwraiths in the Lord of the Rings films, or as the Dementors in the Harry Potter films, the hungry undead, who feed themselves by sucking out a person's soul. These are not just intellectual or

---
iii Bill Street, (2004) *The Astrology of Film*, p.98.

conceptual figures, but evoke a powerful visceral and emotional response, and it is through the medium of film that we encounter them.

Films also expose - literally in projection - the shadow side of the cultural values which exist on the surface. They address powerful emotions such as anger, grief, sadness and depression, and reveal the dark and destructive side of human nature, thus balancing our otherwise relentlessly optimistic, politically correct, cultural values. In Jungian thinking, evil emerges in environments where darkness has been neglected and righteousness has scrubbed clean all traces of shadow. In these situations, the repressed shadow will eventually and inevitably take control. Many films tell the story of the eternal battle between good and evil.

Good films are open to interpretation, unfolding and yielding meaning according to the way we engage with them.[iv] Seeing a film of any significance is not a passive activity. As the lights go down, we allow ourselves to cross the threshold from our daylight consciousness and enter a realm closer to the dream world than to waking life. In the imaginative world we can engage with a wide range of emotions and share a collective ritual experience which can be deeply cathartic. This is analagous to the role of the theatre in ancient Greece, ruled by the god Dionysus and deliberately designed to evoke a powerful collective experience. Rather than being seen as a form of escapism, a flight from reality, theatre and film can draw us more deeply into our lives. They provide a gateway to the deeper reaches of the psyche and feed the soul's hunger for depth.

Some films stir something deep within us, we may find that the emotions evoked will be hard to shake off and will stay with us for some time afterwards. We may need to watch the same film again, sometimes many times, until the emotions have all been used up. This is similar to the psychological technique of amplification - processing in projection - in

---

iv Nancy Cator, (2005) *Cinema and Psyche*, p.1.

which working with a dream by exploring how it might continue to unfold can reveal further insights and deeper meanings.

Astrologers can use myths and stories to breathe life into the paradoxical themes of each axis in the birth chart, and this is where personality theory and a knowledge of character styles can be helpful. They can be used as a way of presenting the whole spectrum of each axis, including its shadow side. And this can lead to increased insight into, and understanding of, the many ways in which the various character styles are expressed in every-day life. Recognising the stories can have a valuable therapeutic function, generating increased flexibility, psychic integration, self-acceptance, modesty and humour.

As such, astrologers can use stories as a way of understanding and describing chart patterns imaginatively rather than diagnostically, mythically rather than medically, as archetypal rather than pathological, as fundamental existential reflections of the human condition, which we all share and can therefore easily relate to.

The following chapters explore just a few of the most recognisable themes which continue to reoccur in stories with human relationships at their core. The stories and films referred to in this book have stood the test of time, and continue to resonate strongly through the generations, evidence that their themes are timeless reflections of human experience. As such, they help to amplify the most common relationship patterns described by the polarities embedded in each axis of the birth chart.

The horoscope is a map of a specific time and place, and the axes reveal the relationship dynamics embedded in that moment, with all their challenges and potential for resolution. But it is the patterns themselves, whether with the same or opposite sex, which are activated in our lives. The gender of the main characters in the following chapters is therefore interchangeable. I have used 'he' when discussing the three positive, yang, sign axes, and 'she' when discussing the three negative, yin, sign axes.

Chapter 4

Cancer/Capricorn: Axis of Incarnation

The Cancer/Capricorn axis

The Cancer/Capricorn axis describes the capacity for emotional give and take, the ability to build safe structures, to self-soothe, to protect and nurture ourselves and others.

As the axis of incarnation, the Cancer/Capricorn axis is ruled by the Moon and Saturn, archetypal symbols for the child and the parent, the contained and the container. It describes our very early needs for physical safety and emotional support. In an individual chart, aspects between the Moon and Saturn, and the signs and houses in which they are placed, provide further information about the nature of the parent/child relationship, as experienced by the child.

The Moon is the child within, geared towards creating and maintaining the emotional bonds which ensure survival, a sense of safety, security and belonging, and the continuity of the family matrix, community or tribe.

Our Moons do not grow up, but Saturn challenges us to do so. The sign of Capricorn, and its ruler Saturn, describe the development of self-reliance, self-control and emotional self-sufficiency, which are necessary if we are to learn to stand on our own feet, and to take care of ourselves and others. Often great providers, common themes on this axis include realism, competence and a strong sense of responsibility. Saturn is the parent within, and people with an emphasis on this axis often take on parenting, caring or protective roles at work, or with friends and family.

Cancer/Capricorn: Axis of Incarnation

Developmental psychology recognises the importance of primal attachment and bonding for a child's optimal physical, emotional, mental and social development. Attachment begins in the womb, when the mother's feelings and behaviour towards her unborn child are absorbed by the baby, develops very quickly in the first few weeks after birth and continues to build during the first nine months of life.

Ideally, both mother and baby will feel safe, secure and relaxed, and the baby will feel welcomed. After birth, if the parent/s are emotionally responsive, calm and understanding, a positive nonverbal emotional exchange can be established. Babies and young children are dependent on tender, supportive and empathic eye contact, facial expression, tone of voice, reassuring body language, and sensitivity to the child's pacing, timing and intensity. Consistent positive emotional exchange engenders in the baby a sense of general wellbeing, and enables the establishment of a secure attachment.

If the baby feels understood, she learns to relax and to trust and, as she adapts to her surroundings, she will thrive. She will interpret the world and other people as an extension of the original bond formed with her mother. The quality of this bond is gradually extended to the quality of the bond with other people and the world.

The Unwanted or Hated Child – and the Schizoid Character Style

Disturbances on this axis are believed to occur if, for whatever reason, the basic security and safety needs of the infant are not adequately met, with the result that the primal mother/child bonding cannot be established. There are, of course, any number of reasons why this may be so. The mother may be anxious, afraid or distracted by problems of her own. She may be in an unsafe or abusive relationship, or her pregnancy may have been unwelcome. The birth process itself may have been deeply traumatic or life-threatening, medically invasive or de-personalised, or the mother may suffer from postnatal depression. It is remarkable how often the experience of early abandonment or actual bereavement occurs on this axis.

Alternatively, the child may have been born into a chaotic family. Her parent/s or primary carers may have been immature, emotionally volatile, out of control or unsafe. A common response is for the child to develop a profound vigilance and, right from the start, to take on the role of trying to parent her parents. This can set the scene for a variety of parenting roles she may adopt in later life, as a way of attempting to soothe, care for and protect herself. She may be terrified of the emotional volatility she experienced in her early environment, and adapt by avoiding strong feelings or anger in herself and others. Becoming prematurely independent and self-sufficient, she withdraws from her immediate environment and builds an internal world to which she can escape. Her outward façade of self-sufficiency often conceals a secret longing to be cared for - but it is too terrifying to allow herself to depend on real people or situations.

Whatever the reasons, with an insecure or absent attachment bond, the baby and very young child experiences her earliest environment, both within and beyond the womb, as cold, neglectful or hostile. She feels rejected, unsafe, unwanted, even hated. If her level of terror is extreme, her core developmental issue becomes one of survival.

It was Wilhelm Reich[i] who first proposed that intense fear, anxiety and tension can be held in the body by what he called 'character armour'. For Reich, muscular armour was a defence that contained the history of the patient's trauma, but also protected the patient from remembering the childhood experiences which had caused the energetic blockages in the first place. In an unsafe world, the body becomes inhibited, rigid or frozen, cut off from spontaneity. There is an inability to relax or feel safe, and a perpetual state of readiness to 'fight' or 'take flight'. The child and emerging adult can appear to be in shock, energetically frozen and emotionally numb,

---

[i] Wilhelm Reich (1897-1957) was an Austrian doctor of medicine and a member of the second generation of psychoanalysts after Sigmund Freud.

misaligned with her environment and out of touch with her body, often unaware whether it is hungry or thirsty, hot or cold. Chronic tension and restricted breathing can be an unconscious response to a threatening and hostile world.

She may deny herself the basic comforts of food and contact with nature, living instead in a 'frozen' state of terror.

The very early message is that the world and other people are the source of pain and rejection, rather than comfort, and therefore cannot be trusted. The unwanted child's emotional reaction is *terror*, although at this stage, provided that the environmental response is modified, her normal healthy development can still proceed. Repair work can still be done, to deepen trust, increase resilience and build emotional bonds. But if it is not modified, then the infant is forced to turn against herself. No young child can bear to be excluded from parental approval and protection, and so she learns to curb her natural impulses, and to treat herself as harshly as she has herself been treated.

Internalising the way she has been treated, the unwanted child comes to believe that there is something wrong with her, that she is damaged or defective in some way, and that she has no right to exist, no permission to incarnate. A common defensive adaptation is to try and become invisible, not wanting to be seen, to hide from herself and others, as a protective measure, in order to avoid further rejection. As she grows up, she may find herself in relationships in which she can hide and not be truly seen or understood.

The absence of human warmth and adequate caretaking results in a kind of disembodied existence. The reality of the isolation, neglect and abandonment she experienced is unbearable, and leads to withdrawal from the world. Close relationships, and particularly conflict, are avoided, and there is an inability to get angry or to face anger in others. Withdrawal represents a safe haven, a way of denying or avoiding emotion, which can lead to a lifelong avoidance of contact with others, and a refusal to allow anyone to get close.

Shifting away from the physical towards the mental or spiritual planes feels safer, and often takes the form of skill specialization, which can be an attempt to try and figure things out intellectually and logically.[1]

The Unwanted Child adapts by learning not to reach out, and retreats instead into his or her own private world. Highly sensitive, her life is spiritualised, intellectualised or fantasized, rather than lived. Typically introspective, her inner world becomes a sanctuary of self-preservation, free from the dangers and anxieties associated with emotional connection to real people and situations. A common defense against what feels like the overwhelming demands of the external world is the tendency to create, and escape into, nostalgic, magical, fantastical or long-lost worlds.[2]

It is remarkable how many academics and writers in these genres have experienced early bereavement, abandonment, cruelty or rejection. Both these professions demand long periods of research and solitude, as well as providing a valid excuse to withdraw from the world. [3]

Workaholism and other addictions can serve as substitutes for human relationships. Adopting a formal or professional role, or identifying with a particular skill can be a way of avoiding emotional contact or intimacy. Having a recognizable role or talent can serve as proof not only that she is not invisible, but that she has a right to exist, and within these roles she can be confident, assertive and effective, in striking contrast to her general shyness and inhibition in social settings. Within the safety of a formal or professional title, she will often take on a parental role, and be exceptionally supportive, nurturing, accepting and understanding of others.

In adult relationships there can be an overwhelming longing for a parental substitute - someone who will never leave us – someone who will care for, protect and even die for us, as a parent will for a child. There can therefore be an attraction to people who appear to represent stability, containment and safety.

Cancer/Capricorn: Axis of Incarnation

This is so important that Richard Idemon[ii] suggested that the prime motivation for up to 90% of all adult relationships is to get our safety and security needs met. As is the case with all the astrological axes, the poles of each axis are mutually dependent. Like all systems, they are self-balancing, so the parent/child roles can be exchanged but not altered. If, for example, the 'parent' in the system is no longer prepared or able to continue in the role of provider and protector, the 'child' will normally respond by re-balancing the system, and in the process discover hitherto undeveloped capabilities, resourcefulness and resilience.

When we choose a parent figure – either consciously or unconsciously – we may be choosing to do some repair work, and maybe to have a family of our own, in an attempt to heal the loneliness we felt as a child. But the chances are that at some point the pattern will be repeated, our primal needs will be disappointed and once again we will feel abandoned in a hostile world. A common infantile response is moodiness, which can be described as unconscious anger and resentment towards the 'parent figure' who fails to pick up our nonverbal signals and fails to anticipate and fulfil all our unspoken needs. Alternatively, apparent emotional self-sufficiency and defensive distancing can be used to mask the level of neediness.

All axes describe a fundamental, developmental double bind. On the Cancer/Capricorn axis there is a longing for friendship, companionship and love, matched only by the terror of reaching out emotionally, which would expose the original vulnerability and risk of rejection.

When this axis polarises, both parties feel abandoned and undernourished. The infant within refuses to grow up and remains needy, dependent, emotionally demanding and increasingly resentful. The 'child' surrenders her own development, refuses to become self-sufficient or responsible, demanding that the 'parent' takes on the role of provider, doing all the work, supporting her financially and emotionally and taking care of

---
ii Richard Idemon, (1992) *Through the Looking Glass*.

all the administrative and domestic aspects of their lives together. But the damage was done many years ago, and the parental substitute can never do enough, so the demands and resentments continue to grow. Alternatively, once the 'child' eventually realises that her partner is incapable of providing the care and protection she needs, she may start searching for another, better, parental substitute, and continue to repeat the same pattern.

In response to these overwhelming demands, and as a method of self-preservation, the 'parent' may cut off her own neediness from consciousness and become increasingly critical, withholding and cold. Withdrawing from the presumed threat or danger of the emotional demands of others, she may become a loner or hermit, neither desiring nor enjoying close relationships and almost always choosing solitary activities. And this makes the 'child' in the system feel even more abandoned. And so the game goes on.

The 'parent' in such a polarised relationship tends to be extremely harsh with herself (an internalisation of her early environment). She may develop rigid self-discipline, an authoritarian character style, and judge, criticise and punish any dependency needs in herself and in others. She may have a lack of empathy, expressed as an apparent emotional detachment, hostility or coldness. Her behaviour may be cynical, callous or even cruel, thus replicating and reinforcing the treatment she received as a child, unaware how it affects other people. It is psychologically true that we tend to treat ourselves and others the same way that we have been treated.[4]

She may also tend to gravitate towards environments which are themselves harsh and punishing, or to relationships with people who are themselves emotionally absent or shut down, or who carry a great deal of anger.

When the Cancer/Capricorn axis becomes polarised, personal fulfilment, creativity, freedom and even happiness are irrelevant – the most important thing is to construct a container in the material world, to which they can belong and within which they can feel safe. And this container can be a family, a business or career, within which they often devote themselves to the care of others, family members, children and animals, work colleagues and communities, often being extremely successful in building businesses and other professional structures. These structures can be a way of gaining respect and recognition in the world, a sense of identity, and, just as important, a feeling of belonging

Social situations and gatherings often cause great anxiety and are avoided whenever possible. People with this character adaptation are normally perfectly capable of presenting themselves as socially available, interested, engaged and involved with others, but at the same time they remain emotionally withdrawn, isolated and apart. This can reveal itself as an apparent indifference to social norms and conventions, a reluctance to reach out for, or accept, well intentioned advice or support, a marked eccentricity and an inner sense of superiority generated by the belief, and relief, that they do not need or have to rely on other people.

People with an emphasis on this axis consider themselves to be observers rather than participants in the world around them. Indeed, they easily feel suffocated if their personal space is violated and need to escape back into their own worlds. They are often unusually sensitive and introspective, preoccupied with their own inner worlds. The only safe relationships are contextual, providing the necessary social or intellectual structures with which to go through the motions of appearing to belong and to be acceptable to others and in the world, as long as these do not require or force the need for emotional intimacy, which they will reject.

A noticeable exception to this rule of withdrawal is the strong bond which is often formed with children and animals, and gentle contact with nature and all living things. These relationships are safe and non-threatening, and people with an emphasis on the Cancer/Capricorn axis are often gifted at nurturing and protecting those in their care, finding great comfort, fulfilment and reassurance in the process.

The secret on this axis is to embrace its tidal nature. Just as the tide ebbs and flows under the influence of the Moon, there will be times when the tide is coming in and the emotions are flowing outwards, all generous, caring and supportive towards those in their care. Equally, there will be times when the tide is going out, the emotions are withdrawn, and retreat, privacy and self-protection become necessary.

Cancer/Capricorn Stories

Many of the stories relevant on this axis concern historical themes, family and tribal sagas, and tales of early abandonment, rejection, loneliness and isolation. Such stories provide a safe and often therapeutic vehicle for getting in touch with the sadness felt by the orphan within.[5] These stories are often about rites of passage, from psychological childhood and dependency, through a painful transition during which the main character suffers the abandonment or death of a parent or parental figure, and finally to psychological adulthood.

Often the object of love in these stories is someone who has died. Many stories trace the painful separation of a bereaved person from their loved one, and the profound grief and mourning which follows, before they are ready to let go and move forward.[6]

Once sufficient parenting has been experienced, one or both of the pair may realise that their partner is not the one they choose to be with for the rest of their lives. Ultimately, the archetypal parent/child system is transitional, rather than lifelong. Eventually the parent or parental substitute will have served their purpose and provided us with a sufficiently safe and protective environment, helping us grow in confidence and independence until we are ready to move on, which is, after all, the core function and purpose of the parental role.

Re-visiting these stories can be a way of coming to terms with the pain of primal abandonment. They provide an opportunity to mourn at last for the loss of the illusion that we ever had the adequate support or love we needed to enable our real self to emerge out into the world. Their therapeutic value is to help us to feel at last and, as the feelings come to the surface, to mourn, and to release the underlying grief, depression and even rage, along with the tears which have been locked up for so many years. Gradually, the long-standing melancholy, characterized by withdrawal, nostalgia or moodiness, can begin to fall away. Although we cannot change what happened in the past, with the emergence of a more adult adaptation to the world, we learn at last to stand on our own feet, develop compassion for ourselves and learn to nurture and love the child within.

Peter Pan

The story of **Peter Pan**, written as a play in 1904 by J.M. Barrie, has appeared in numerous adaptations, sequels, and prequels since then, including the 1953 Disney animated feature film, various stage musicals, live-action feature films,[iii] TV series and video games. The universal and consistent appeal of this story indicates the timeless relevance of its themes.

Figure 1 Peter Pan

Peter Pan was a boy who refused to grow up. When his parents had another child and forgot about him, he ran away to the magical realm of Neverland, where he was the leader of the Lost Boys, a band of infants who had fallen out of their prams and were never claimed by their parents. They were all orphans, a central theme which continues throughout the story, along with the fear of growing up.

Wendy was the oldest child in the Darling family, with two younger brothers. One night, she woke up to find Peter sitting on the floor, in tears.

---

iii *Hook* (1991), *Peter Pan* (2003) and the story of J.M. Barrie, *Finding Neverland* (2004).

Star Crossed: Astrology, Personality Theory and the Meeting of Opposites

He was crying because his shadow wouldn't stick to him. In other words, he had no substance. Spirits and sprites do not have shadows because they do not exist in the real world. When Wendy sewed his shadow to the tips of his shoes, Peter was delighted.

He persuaded Wendy to fly with him to Neverland and to be his mother there. She agreed, but only if she could also take John and Michael with her, whom she was already looking after. They flew to Neverland, where Wendy met the Lost Boys, all of whom also wanted Wendy to be their mother. She took care of the boys by day, and told them stories at night, in their cosy house under the woods.

Neverland is populated by indians, mermaids and pirates. From a psychological viewpoint, they were all imaginative figures belonging to Peter Pan's inner world. The most interesting figure is Captain Hook – a shadow figure who, tellingly, is pursued by time, and with it the fear of old age and death. Death itself is symbolised as a crocodile who had swallowed a clock. Crocodiles are known to drown and bury their prey in the river banks, waiting for them to rot. As a creature of the air, Peter is not only afraid of his emotions and feelings, but also terrified of being dragged down into the unconscious depths. Eventually, after a series of adventures, Captain Hook is eaten by his nemesis, the crocodile, and Peter returns with Wendy and her brothers to their home. Wendy's parents offer to adopt Peter Pan and the Lost Boys, but Peter chooses to stay in Neverland, where he will never have to grow up.

The **Peter Pan syndrome** is a term used in pop-psychology to describe an adult who is socially immature[iv]. The musician Michael Jackson closely identified with Peter Pan, and in 2003 he told the interviewer Martin Bashir, "I am Peter Pan". Bashir said, "No, you're Michael Jackson". Jackson then replied, "I'm Peter Pan in my heart". Jackson, of course, named his fantastical home "Neverland Ranch".

---

iv A term used since the publication of the book by Dr Dan Kiley: *The Peter Pan Syndrome: Men Who Have Never Grown Up,* 1983.

J.M. Barrie

J.M. Barrie was a journalist, playwright and author of children's books, including *Peter Pan*. He had Cancer/Capricorn on his ASC/DES axis, with Venus rising in Cancer and the Moon on the DES in Capricorn. His life and relationships reveal many of the Cancer/Capricorn themes.

Figure 2 JM Barrie

His story was told in the film *Finding Neverland* (2004), starring Johnny Depp (Moon, South Node in Capricorn, North Node in Cancer) and Kate Winslett (MC/IC Cancer/Capricorn). By all accounts, J.M. Barrie's father was cold and distant, and did not interact at all with his nine children, of whom James was the eighth. When James was six years old, his older brother David, and his mother's favourite, died in a skating accident, a loss from which his mother never recovered. James tried in vain to replace his lost brother in his mother's affections, but was rejected, an event which was to mark the rest of his life. He nevertheless published an adoring biography of his mother after her death. Growing up shy and sensitive, Barrie became a writer, a socially sanctioned way of retreating into his imagination and creating his own, safe, fantasy land. He married the actress Mary Ansell in 1894 and they began taking walks with their dog in Kensington Gardens, a park near their London home, where Barrie became a favourite of the children brought there by their nannies, entertaining them with his antics and stories about pirates and fairies. In a hostile world, the safest relationships are with animals and children, who will never reject or abandon you.

The children Barrie was fondest of were the young sons of Arthur and Sylvia Llewelyn Davies, George, Jack, Peter, Michael and Nico. The stories he told them became the basis for his 1904 play *Peter Pan, or The Boy Who Would Not Grow Up,* which became a huge hit in Britain and the US.

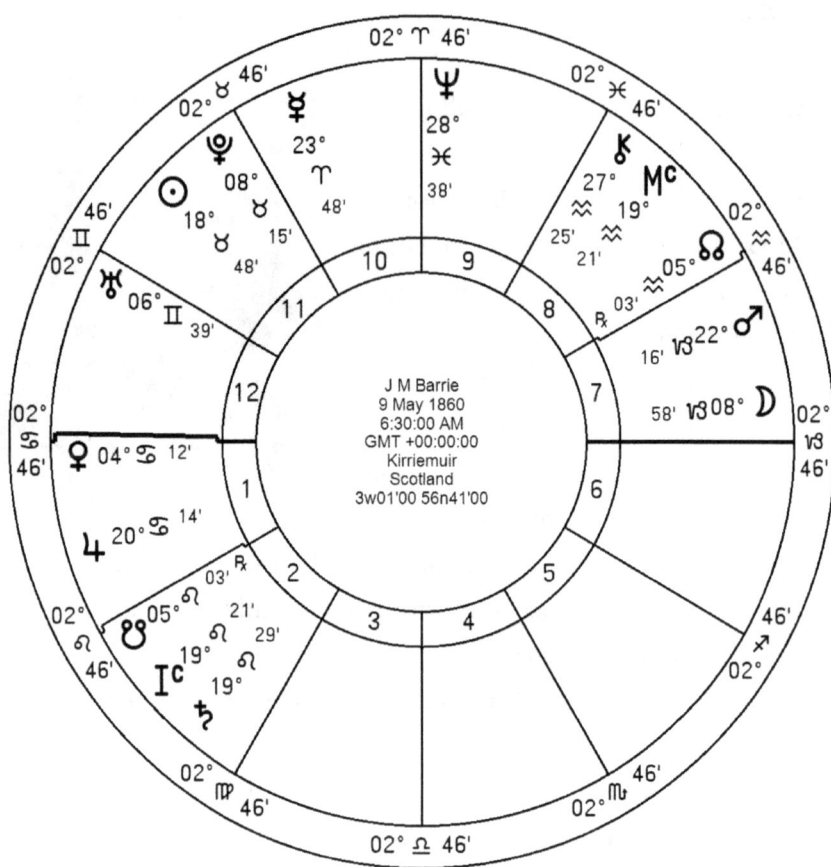

Barrie's marriage was an unhappy one, cold and formal and, by many accounts, sexless. It was certainly childless, although Mary was anxious for a child. She began an affair in 1909 with the writer Gilbert Cannan, and the marriage ended in divorce.

Barrie remained close to the Llewelyn Davies family. When Arthur and Sylvia died of cancer within a few years of each other, he became the guardian and surrogate father to the boys. Both George and Michael predeceased him. George was killed in action in 1915 during World War I, and Michael drowned while he was at Oxford in 1921. Twenty three years after Barrie's death in June 1937, Peter, who had become a successful publisher, committed suicide by throwing himself under a London underground train.

Notes

1 The brilliant, reclusive and socially awkward code breaker Alan Turing was the subject of the film *The Imitation Game (2014)*, starring Benedict Cumberbatch. Benedict Cumberbatch is also known for his film roles portraying other exceptionally gifted and often eccentric intellectuals, such as *Sherlock Holmes* and as Julian Assange, who came to international attention as the founder of the whistle-blowing website WikiLeaks *(The Fifth Estate,* 2013*)*. Alan Turing, Benedict Cumberbatch and Julian Assange all have Sun and Mercury in Cancer.

2 The French author Marcel Proust is a good example. Proust had Saturn conjunct MC in Capricorn, with Jupiter, IC, Mercury, Sun and Uranus in Cancer. He is best known for his monumental seven-volume novel *À la recherche du temps perdu* (*Remembrance of Things Past*). Another famously reclusive figure was the Swedish-American actress Greta Garbo, one of the 20th century's most famous and iconic Hollywood film stars. Garbo had the Capricorn/Cancer axis on her MC/IC, with Uranus in Capricorn. She also belonged to the generation which had Neptune in nostalgic Cancer.

From the early days of her career, Garbo avoided publicity. She never signed autographs or answered fan mail, and never appeared at Oscar ceremonies, even when she was nominated. She explained in an interview that her desire for privacy began when she was a child, stating, "As early as I can remember, I have wanted to be alone. I detest crowds, don't like many people." She is closely associated with a quote from the film *Grand Hotel*, in which she said: "I want to be alone; I just want to be alone". In retirement, Garbo gave an interview in which she described her struggle with her many eccentricities, and her life-long melancholy and moodiness.

3 Rudyard Kipling, who wrote *The Jungle Book, Kim* and the *Just So* stories, is a fine example. His chart has a Sun Jupiter conjunction in Capricorn in the 4th house, opposite Uranus in Cancer in the 10th house. C.S. Lewis, who wrote the *Chronicles of Narnia,* was a close friend of J.R.R. Tolkien, who wrote *The Hobbit* and *The Lord of the Rings*. Lewis Carroll was a lecturer in mathematics at Oxford for early 30 years, and wrote *'Alice's Adventures in Wonderland (1865)* and *Through the Looking Glass (1871)*. All three were academics and Fellows of Oxford colleges for many years, an environment which enabled them to retreat from the world, while ensuring that all their domestic needs were provided for.

Star Crossed: Astrology, Personality Theory and the Meeting of Opposites

4 Charles Dickens' *A Christmas Carol* is a classic Cancer/Capricorn story. The novella begins on Christmas Eve with Ebenezer Scrooge, a mean and miserly man working in his counting-house. His clerk, Bob Cratchit, is trying to warm himself over a candle, since Scrooge refuses to give him more coal. Scrooge's cheerful nephew, Fred, arrives to wish him a Merry Christmas and to invite his uncle to a Christmas dinner. Scrooge refuses the invitation and sends his nephew packing. He is then approached by two charity collectors, collecting for the poor and homeless. He refuses to give them a donation, claiming that the prisons and workhouses should provide for the poor, or that they should die 'and decrease the surplus population'.

Later that night, Scrooge has a series of visions, in which he is haunted by the ghosts of Christmas Past, Present and Future, who show him how his mean and withholding behaviour has affected those around him. The ghost of Christmas Past shows Scrooge scenes from his past engagement to Belle, who leaves him because he seems to love money more than her. He is upset to see that Belle is now a happy woman with a family of her own. The ghost of Christmas Present takes Scrooge to the home of the Cratchit family where he is saddened to see their poverty, and their sick son, Tiny Tim. The ghost of Christmas Yet to Come shows Scrooge the death of Tiny Tim, and leads him to a gravestone which bears his own name.

When Scrooge awakes on Christmas Day, he is relieved and delighted to discover that these visions were all dreams. There is still time for him to change, and he immediately buys a prize turkey which he delivers to the Cratchits, makes a donation to the charity collectors on the street, goes to church, and finally to his nephew's house for Christmas dinner. The following day, he offers Bob Cratchit a pay rise and promises to help look after his family.

Charles Dickens never forgot his unhappy, poverty-stricken childhood and used his memories to write about the immense wrongs of the Victorian period. His book *Oliver Twist* is based on his experiences during that time. As an adult, he was a moody man and, despite growing wealth and fame, he worried continually about money. Dickens had Mercury and Saturn in Capricorn, with Mercury ruling both his ASC and MC axes.

5 People with an emphasis of planets on the Cancer/Capricorn axis feel more comfortable as observers of life, rather than participants. As such, they tend to be attracted to historical, family and tribal sagas, such as *Downton Abbey*, *The Crown* and even *Game of Thrones*, which explore the dramas and emotional highs and lows of family or tribal systems from which they have felt excluded. The tragic story of *Romeo and Juliet* is a good example; *The Sound of Music*, in which Maria and Baron von Trapp eventually heal their wounds of loneliness and create a happy family, is a perennial favourite.

6 The 1990 films *Ghost* (Patrick Swayze and Demi Moore) and *Truly Madly Deeply* (Juliet Stephenson and Alan Rickman), are fine examples.

Other stories on this axis portray rites of passage from psychological childhood and dependency to adulthood. In *The Bodyguard* (1992), Kevin Costner is the parent figure, the protector, and Whitney Houston takes the role of the child, the one in need of protection. Costner first came to fame in the film *Dances with Wolves* (1990), and in real life he is described as being a perfectionist, hard worker, determined, cool and private. Kevin Costner's nodal axis is in Cancer (South Node)/Capricorn (North Node). In addition he has a Sun/Chiron conjunction in Capricorn opposite a Jupiter/Uranus conjunction in Cancer.

Actors often seem to be drawn to play characters which reflect their own character styles. Dustin Hoffman, for example, has played many roles concerned with loneliness, abandonment and alienation from the family. One of his most famous films is, of course, *The Graduate* (1967) – a significant rite of passage film in which we see him on the painful pivot of regression back into the family – the substitute mother, in this case Mrs Robinson – or developing the courage to reach out into an adult relationship. In other films, such as *Rainman* (1988), *Midnight Cowboy* (1969), *Kramer vs Kramer* (1979) and *Tootsie* (1982), he plays people who are alienated, rejected, or outsiders. His role in *Good Will Hunting* (1997) is a particularly powerful example of these themes. Dustin Hoffman's ASC/DES axis is Capricorn/Cancer. He has Jupiter in Capricorn on the ASC and Venus/Pluto in Cancer.

Chapter 5

Taurus/Scorpio: The Axis of Exchange

The Taurus/Scorpio axis is ruled by Venus and Mars (Pluto) and is naturally associated with the balancing principles of the second and eighth houses. As a fixed axis, the themes of physical, material and emotional resources and their exchange are always intense. At root, they describe the natural biological rhythms of incorporation and elimination, retention and release.

The gentle, peace-loving and sensuous sign of Taurus, ruled by Venus, seeks safety and stability, and describes the simple, biological and emotional drive towards incorporation. The balancing sign of Scorpio, ruled by Mars and Pluto, ensures that any stagnancy or over-retention is regularly broken down, purged and eliminated, in the service of the continuance of organic growth and new life.

A well-balanced Taurus/Scorpio axis describes a sound sense of self-worth, a fixity of purpose, the ability to provide emotionally and materially for ourselves and others, a pride in our accomplishments and the courage to defend ourselves and our values when necessary. At best, this axis describes the ability to trust the organic flow of life, that there will be times of emotional and material accumulation and times when any toxicity needs to be purged in order to re-establish a healthy equilibrium. In balance, this axis can bring confidence and strength, an exceptional ability to manage resources, and an intuitive understanding of the organic cycles of life which is often associated with the gift of healing.

Developmental psychology recognises the power and urgency of the infant's early physical and emotional demands. If the infant's instinctive and valid needs for nurture and nourishment are adequately and consistently fulfilled, then she can pass through this stage with a healthy sense of entitlement, self-confidence and a fundamental trust in life. She will experience her world as bountiful, rewarding, enjoyable and safe. If the child has been respected and valued in her own right, she will have a good sense of self-worth. Knowing what she needs and what is right for her, she will not be afraid to ask, or even to demand, knowing that, at root, life is benign and supportive, and that her appetites can be satisfied since there is plenty for everyone. As she grows up, and into adulthood, she will have the confidence to engage fully with the passion and intensity, and the give and take of close relationships.

The Abandoned Child – and the Oral Character Style

It is believed that an oral character style is formed when, for whatever reason, the child's very early demands for nurture, nourishment and emotional attunement are inconsistently, inadequately or only partially met. The child has tasted something of what she needs but, because her needs were never fully met, her appetites were never fully satisfied; she is left with a deep-seated feeling of emptiness, a voracious, gnawing hunger, which she continues to seek to fill. Whether or not this emotional or physical abandonment is literally true, the very early experience on this axis is a deep-seated psychology of 'not-enoughness' – that something very important has been withheld or denied before we were ready to move on.

Like the Cancer/Capricorn axis, the *oral phase* is believed to relate to the very early developmental period of attachment and bonding. But the *abandoned child* finds herself in an even more painful position than the *unwanted child* of the Cancer/Capricorn axis, whose defensive adaptation involves learning not to reach out, but to retreat mentally and physically from the terror of the hostile environment she originally experienced.

The abandoned child comes to believe that her needs will always be denied, or are too great to be satisfied. The result is a chronic core experience of deprivation and, as is the case with the very young child whose survival depends on others, she continues to seek what she needs from the outside world and from other people. The developmental issue will be one of need, and the emotional reaction is chronic resentment and irritation, beneath which lies voracious rage, which is pushed firmly into the unconscious.

As with all character styles, our conscious attitudes and beliefs tend to be the polar opposite of our unconscious attitudes and beliefs. If the Taurus/Scorpio axis becomes radically split or dissociated, this sets the scene for a series of battles for possession and ownership of what are believed to be limited resources. Power struggles will be triggered which have survival issues at their core. They often concern sexual possessiveness, battles over money or shared resources, ownership, values and possessions, both personal and shared.

The development of an oral character style can lead to one or both of two major adaptations. On one end of this axis is **voracious hunger**, where we continue to seek in the 'other', a partner or parental substitute, someone who will fulfil all our needs and finally heal our primal experience of deprivation. But, like the mythic figure Tantalus, our hunger and thirst are insatiable, since nothing and nobody will ever be enough. The despair of unfulfilled emptiness is endlessly acquisitive and can lead to taking, or helping oneself, to other people, or their possessions. On the other end of this axis is the *caretaker* or *provider*, who adapts by seeking to provide for, support and sustain others, but from a position of emptiness.

People with an oral adaptation consciously seek others who they believe will be supportive, nurturing and safe but, with an inadequately developed sense of their own intrinsic value or worth, they remain dependent on them for their self-esteem. This can lead to extreme possessiveness and an attempt to incorporate the other, body, mind and soul. Having given away their power, they naturally feel that they are owed something in return, but it will never be enough.

Unconsciously, they anticipate a re-occurrence of the original abandonment and, in spite of their best intentions, almost as soon as a relationship is formed, they start searching for signs of rejection or waning affection. With such a great investment, it is not surprising that before long, intense feelings of jealousy, suspicion and insecurity emerge. They may become preoccupied with unjustified doubts regarding the fidelity of their spouse or sexual partner. Any imagined minor slight or withdrawal by the loved one triggers intense anxiety or jealousy.

As they try to get their partner to meet their insatiable demands, they may become increasingly controlling, obsessive and devouring, to the point where the partner is no longer allowed a separate life and effectively becomes a prisoner in the relationship, subjected to constant surveillance. They are effectively being stalked. Any friendships, achievements or activities which the partner has outside the relationship are viewed with suspicion and irrational jealousy.

An example would be when a person is on the phone every few minutes, asking where their partner is now, if their partner loves them, how much they love them, who are they with, when will they be home, and all manner of demands until they become so emotionally invasive that they eventually ensure, in the face of such impossible demands, that they will be rejected again. The end result is often violent. In extreme cases, the underlying *primal rage* can emerge with terrifying power, making this one of the most potentially violent of the personality types. Most of all, obsessive lovers want to cleanse themselves of the rage they felt towards their withholding parents. Caught between suspicion and dependency, at one moment they can be hurling accusations at their partner, and at the next moment apologising profusely, in an attempt to avoid a repetition of the primal abandonment.

It is difficult for the partner to believe that their civilised, adapted, well adjusted, caring partner has turned into a jealous monster who won't let them out of their sight. Initially, it is usual to interpret another person's need and dependency as proof of how much we are loved and cared for, but it is in fact a devouring and voracious possessiveness which bears no relation at all to genuine love.

Paranoid feelings can also extend beyond personal relationships to a pervasive mistrust and suspicion of the motives of others. People on this axis may suspect, without sufficient basis, that others are exploiting, harming or deceiving them. They may be doubtful about the loyalty or trustworthiness of friends, associates or partners, and reluctant to confide in others because of unwarranted fears that the information will be used maliciously against them. They may interpret benign remarks or events as personally threatening or demeaning, and be quick to react angrily or counter-attack.

Many of the Taurus/Scorpio themes can be related back to the original experience of oral deprivation, and can lead to a kind of psychic cannibalism. A pattern or habit of indiscriminate stealing, hoarding, storing and even burying can be established in an attempt to gain control over what are believed to be limited resources.

On the other end of the Taurus/Scorpio spectrum, the *caretaker* or *provider* adaptation normally occurs if the parent/s were themselves excessively needy, possessive or controlling, in which case the infant's valid personal boundaries may have been violated rather than respected. The child finds herself in a painful double bind, in which her own needs for safety, security and consistency are unmet, but she is simultaneously expected to fulfil the needs and demands of her parent/s. If the parents and/or caretakers are physically, emotionally or even psychically invasive, she feels disempowered, at their mercy, with no alternative but to surrender to their demands, which sets the scene for similar relationships in adulthood. The child learns to deny or reject her own neediness, and becomes unwilling or unable to reach out to others or ask for help, for fear of being further exploited. She becomes unable to take in, to incorporate or to receive any support from others.

Taurus/Scorpio: The Axis of Exchange

Instead, she adapts to constantly meet the needs of others at her own expense in the hope of gaining their love. She may develop an exaggerated sense of responsibility, and take on the role of *provider* or *caretaker*. The caretaker would do anything to avoid revealing weakness or neediness, and will see herself as all-nurturing, all-giving and all-generous, providing others with what she never received for herself. In this way, she hopes to get her needs met vicariously, but it is always resentful and demands something in return. Whether consciously or not, this adaptation is designed to engender the dependency of the other, to protect against a repetition of the original abandonment. With this strategy in place there is a high price to pay for the recipients of all this generosity, who find themselves increasingly disempowered and controlled.

But there is an equally high price to pay for the *provider*. Operating from a place of 'not enoughness', she lacks the ability to self-sooth or self-nurture and can become worn out by the heavy responsibilities she has taken on, which are more than she can sustain. The *caretaker* can often be recognised by her self-deprivation, poor self-care, and exhaustion, which can lead to periods of physical collapse, illness or depression.

The challenge on this axis is to recognise that it is impossible to prevent what has already happened in our early childhood. The continued search for the 'lost mother' is in fact the search for the fantasy of a relationship which never existed in the first place. Insatiable demands for unconditional support and nurturing are too much to expect, and inappropriate for adult functioning. If we can learn to face our own adult sense of aloneness, we can develop the ability to relinquish, to let go of, and mourn, the painful and useless dependency on others to fulfil our needs. Ultimately, it is possible to develop sufficient self esteem to value, care for, nurture and provide both materially and emotionally for ourselves.

Star Crossed: Astrology, Personality Theory and the Meeting of Opposites

Taurus/Scorpio Stories

The Taurus/Scorpio axis provides an extremely rich theme in stories, myths and films. It concerns the overwhelming and obsessive need for control and power over another person, and its inevitable consequences, generated by an unfulfilled and unfulfillable primal hunger for emotional connection. The film *Fatal Attraction* is a well-known version of this archetypal story.[1]

Relationships on this theme typically describe how one person becomes the sole focus of another's existence, and how everything else falls away. The protagonist pursues the object of their desire, trying to make themselves needed in an effort to keep the other from leaving. But the more desperate they get, the more they are pushed away, until a final rejection ends their denial of the other's disinterest, and they are filled with a terrifying rage.

It is recognised that, as a general rule, women tend to turn their anger inwards, against themselves. They are more likely than men to become self-destructive, to self-harm, to turn their need for control to food - as in cases of anorexia and bulimia - or to become consumed by obsessive thoughts. Sometimes women in this situation may try to kill themselves, not only because of their pain but also as an act of revenge - to show the world that he is her murderer.

Men in the grip of similar situations tend to turn their anger outwards and vent their anger against their rejecters, as in most cases of domestic violence. They are more likely to turn their partners into prisoners, cutting them off from other relationships and subjecting them to constant surveillance. Statistically, it is estimated that well over half of all murdered women are killed by partners they left or tried to leave.

The Story of Bluebeard

Bluebeard is a French fairy tale first published in 1697, and is a classic example of a polarised Taurus/Scorpio relationship, with the male as the protagonist. At least thirty operas and over twenty films have been written on the Bluebeard theme, such as Hitchcock's *Notorious*. The theme is also used in Stephen King's novel *The Shining* (1977). The feminist author and psychologist Clarissa Pinkola Estes describes the psychological symbolism of the Bluebeard story in her book *Women Who Run With The Wolves* (1996). The tale tells the story of a violent nobleman in the habit of murdering his wives and the attempts of one wife to escape the fate of her predecessors.

Figure 3 Bluebeard, his wife and the magical key, Gustave Dore 19th Century illustration

Bluebeard was a wealthy aristocrat, feared because of his ugliness and avoided by all. Although he had been married several times, no one knew what had become of his wives. However, he managed to persuade Fatima, the daughter of one of his neighbours, to marry him, and after the ceremony she went to live with him in his castle. By all accounts, she was seduced by his wealth and power.

Shortly afterwards, Bluebeard announced that he had to go away for a while; he gave all the keys of the castle to his new wife, including the key to one small room that she was forbidden to enter. Almost immediately after his departure, she was overcome with the desire to see what the forbidden room held, and finally her visiting sister convinced her to satisfy her curiosity and open the door.

Fatima immediately discovered the room's horrible secret: its floor was awash with blood, and the dead bodies of her husband's former wives hung from hooks on the walls. Horrified, she locked the door, but the key had become covered with blood which would not wash off. When Bluebeard returned he knew immediately what his wife had done. In a blind rage he threatened to behead her on the spot, and so she locked herself in the highest tower with her sister. While Bluebeard, sword in hand, tried to break down the door, the sisters awaited the arrival of their two brothers. At the last moment, the brothers broke into the castle, and as Bluebeard attempted to flee, they killed him.

From a psychological viewpoint, all the characters in this story are aspects of Fatima's psyche. Clarissa Pinkola Estes writes that Fatima plays out the very human story of a naïve and inadequately parented young woman who is unaware that she is, in fact, prey. She is seduced by the promise of power and wealth, and even unconsciously drawn to engage with her inner predator. Relevant parallels can be drawn to the events which led to the recent 'Me Too' movement, and many other examples of the exploitation and sexual grooming of young girls and women by powerful men.

As always in fairy stories, it is the actions of Fatima's sister and brothers, those inner mercurial figures, who help her to see what is actually happening, to gain perspective and detachment, and deliver her from the predator within her own psyche.[2]

The Story of Beauty and the Beast

Another popular and enduring fairy tale which illuminates the themes on this axis is *Beauty and the Beast,* originally published in 1740. Unlike the story of Bluebeard, this story has a happy ending. It describes the achievement of balance in the Taurus/Scorpio axis. Both characters have sufficient levels of self worth, the ability to love, and to surrender power and control over the other, which leads to the happy conclusion of the story. It was Jung who wrote, "Where love rules, there is no will to power, and where power predominates, love is lacking. The one is the shadow of the other."

Beauty is initially betrayed by her father, who exchanges his most precious possession, his daughter, for his own freedom. Significantly, the Beast insists that Beauty must come to his castle of her own accord. On her arrival, he receives her graciously and informs her that she is mistress of the castle and that he is her servant.

Eventually she becomes homesick and the Beast allows her to return home, on condition that she returns a week later. The ability of the Beast to release Beauty indicates that he is capable of loving her, of relinquishing his power and control over her, albeit for a short time. Beauty sets off for home with an enchanted mirror, which allows her to see what is going on back at the Beast's castle, and a ring, which allows her to return to the castle in an instant when turned three times around her finger.

Her sisters, who in this instance represent the shadow side of the Taurus/Scorpio axis, are jealous when they hear of her happy life, and conspire to delay her promised return to the castle. In this story, the sisters are exposed as greedy and vengeful, only capable of using others to get what they want. After some time, Beauty uses the enchanted mirror and is horrified to discover that the Beast is lying half-dead of heartbreak. She immediately uses the ring to return to him. She tells the Beast that she loves him and, as her tears fall on him, he is transformed into a handsome prince. As so often in fairy stories, it transpires that a curse had been put on the prince, only to be broken if, despite his apparent ugliness, he could find true love. Like all good fairy stories, Beauty and the Beast live happily ever after.

Star Crossed: Astrology, Personality Theory and the Meeting of Opposites

Pablo Picasso

Pablo Picasso's birth chart has an extremely strong Taurus/Scorpio axis. He has Chiron and a four-planet stellium in Taurus in the 10th house, Saturn, Neptune, Jupiter and Pluto, opposite Sun and Mercury in Scorpio. The Sun in Scorpio is the ruler of the chart, and the planetary rulers of both the Taurus/Scorpio and MC/IC axis, Venus and Mars, are square to each other.

Figure 4 Pablo Picasso

It is not unusual for male artists to draw obsessively on the faces and bodies of their wives and lovers for inspiration and Picasso was no exception.

Picasso had a complicated relationship with women. The most important women in his life were catalysts in his development as an artist. During his long career, each represents the evolution of different styles and visual languages. Twice married, he typically had ongoing relationships with several women at the same time. Just as they became obsessively involved with him, so he became dependent on them.

In tens of thousands of paintings, drawings and prints, he explored his passion for them, attempting to capture not just the way they looked, but the totality of his feelings towards them. Picasso's sexuality fuelled his art and, alongside images of great tenderness, he eviscerated many of his women, painting them pulled and gouged into tortured shapes, women cut in bits and reconfigured on the canvas.

Loyal, generous and affectionate when it suited him, Picasso could be brutal to friends, lovers and even complete strangers. "Women are machines for suffering," Picasso told his mistress Françoise Gilot in 1943.

Taurus/Scorpio: The Axis of Exchange

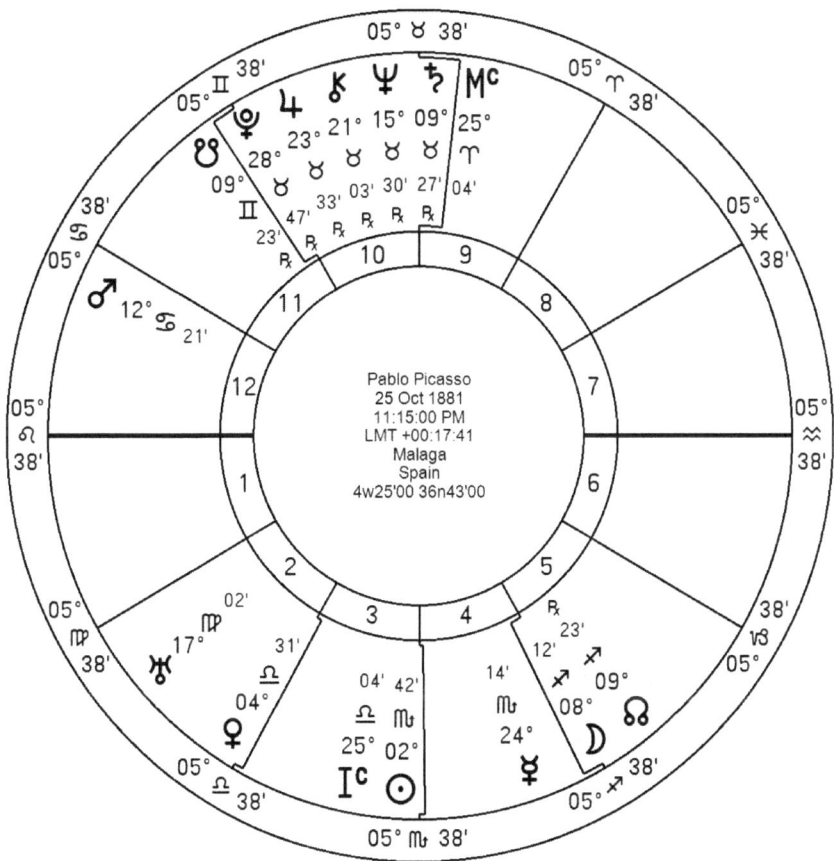

As they embarked on their nine-year affair, the 61-year-old artist warned the 21-year-old student: "For me there are only two kinds of women, goddesses and doormats".

In her memoir, *Picasso, My Grandfather*, **Marina Picasso** writes of his treatment of women, "He submitted them to his animal sexuality, tamed them, bewitched them, ingested them, and crushed them onto his canvas. After he had spent many nights extracting their essence, once they were bled dry, he would dispose of them."

Of the several important women in his life, two, Marie-Thérése Walter, and his second wife, Jacqueline Roque, committed suicide. Others, notably his first wife Olga Khokhlova, and his mistress Dora Maar, had succumbed to nervous breakdowns.

Notes

1 The film *Fatal Attraction* describes the events which unfold when the Taurus/Scorpio axis becomes radically polarized. In this version, the woman is the protagonist. At the beginning of the film we meet two apparently mature, well adapted, rational, professionally successful adults, Dan, played by Michael Douglas, and Alex, played by Glenn Close. They believe they are perfectly capable of conducting an affair without disrupting their lives. But as soon as the relationship is formed, Dan becomes the sole focus of Alex's existence. She believes that her very survival depends on him, and becomes ever more obsessed, demanding and needy, to the extent of self-harming. She slashes her wrists to try to bind him to her with guilt. In other words, the voracious rage of the oral stage is unleashed with all the force of the 18-month-old child who is incapable at that stage of any kind of rationalisation. Her demands and efforts to control him cause him to pull back and try to end the relationship. She refuses to accept his withdrawal, convincing herself that she can win him back. She is obsessed with the fantasy of a relationship which never really existed in the first place. The more desperate she gets, the more he pushes her away until a final rejection finally ends her denial of his disinterest. Now she is filled with a rage which she directs towards him and his family, in escalating degrees. She begins to stalk him, destroys his car with acid, invades his home, kidnaps his daughter and boils the daughter's pet rabbit on the stove. Finally she tries to stab him to death with a large butcher's knife, a scenario which ends with her own death.

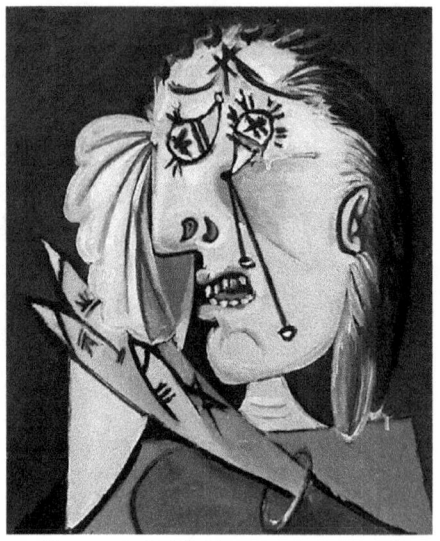

Figure 5 Pablo Picasso portrait of Dora Maar
La femme qui pleure
(Weeping woman) 1937

Actors are often drawn to films which reflect their own charts. For example, Glenn Close has Pluto conjunct ASC, and the Taurus/Scorpio axis on her MC/IC, with Chiron in Scorpio. Michael Douglas was also well qualified to play this role, with Taurus/Scorpio on his ASC/DES axis, square Pluto, and their rulers, Venus

Taurus/Scorpio: The Axis of Exchange

and Mars, conjunct in Libra, square Saturn in Cancer in the eighth house. Similar themes are evident in other Michael Douglas films, such as the *War of the Roses*, *Basic Instinct*, *Disclosure*, *A Perfect Murder* and *Falling Down*.

Jeremy Irons is another actor who seems to be drawn to films of this nature, such as *Lolita*, *Kafka* and *Damage*. With a Taurus/Scorpio nodal axis, Jeremy Irons has Mars and Chiron in Scorpio in the 4th house, and a Venus Pluto conjunction on the ASC in Leo.

Damage tells the story of a married man who becomes so obsessively involved with his son's fiancée that he pursues her without regard for the consequences. The affair destroys many lives but many years later he sees her by chance in an airport, and finally recognises that his obsessive love for her was based on an image of her that he created in his own imagination.

2 The Bluebeard theme is repeated in many stories and films, such as the figure of Hannibal Lector in *Silence of the Lambs*, played by Anthony Hopkins, whose MC/IC axis is Scorpio/Taurus. But there are many chilling real-life examples of extreme pathology in this psychological dynamic. The Joseph Fritzl case emerged in 2008, when a woman reported to the police that she had been held captive for 24 years behind eight locked doors in the basement area of the family house by her father, Josef, who had consistently assaulted, sexually abused and raped her, resulting in the birth of seven children. Four of the children remained in captivity with their mother, while the other three were raised by Fritzl and his wife, having been reported as foundlings. Josef Fritzl has Venus in Taurus opposite Jupiter in Scorpio, sextile and trine to Pluto in Cancer. Mars is in Libra opposite Sun in Aries.

Possessiveness and ownership of the bodies of their victims is a common theme of serial killers with an emphasis on this axis. Dennis Nilsen was a British serial killer and necrophiliac, who murdered at least twelve young men in London in a series of killings committed between 1978 and 1983. Nilsen's victims were strangled, and then ritually bathed and dressed. He would keep their bodies with him for extended periods of time, before dissecting and disposing of their remains by burning them or flushing them down a lavatory. Dennis Nilsen has Taurus/Scorpio on his ASC/DES axis, with Venus, the chart ruler, in Scorpio on the DES, square Pluto.

Frederick 'Fred' West was an English serial killer who murdered at least 12 young women over 20 years, between 1967 and 1987 in Gloucestershire, England, the majority with his second wife, Rosemary. The murders involved rape, bondage, torture and mutilation, and the victims' bodies were typically buried in the cellar or garden of the Wests' home, which became known as "the House of Horrors". Fred West had Venus in Scorpio and Saturn in Taurus closely conjunct Uranus. His Mars is in Aries on the DES square Moon in Capricorn in the 4th house.

Chapter 6

Gemini/Sagittarius: The Axis of Exploration

The mutable Gemini/Sagittarius axis is ruled by Mercury and Jupiter. It describes our drive to learn and our sense of adventure, the urge to make new connections and to grow beyond what we already know. This axis of exploration describes the relationship between our immediate environment and the wider world, between learning and teaching, the student and the mentor, information and meaning, facts and knowledge, and education generally. Psychologically, it represents the instinctive and natural desire to grow beyond the primal parent/child system, and the equal fear of doing so. On the Gemini/Sagittarius axis we look outwards, rather than inwards, and we continue to seek to learn, grow and expand our worlds through our connections with others.

Charts in which these themes come to life are those with the Ascendant/Descendant, MC/IC, nodal axis or several planets on the Gemini/Sagittarius axis or in the third and ninth houses. The signs and houses in which Mercury and Jupiter are placed, and any aspects between them, provide more specific, detailed information.

For people with the angles, nodes or several planets across the Gemini/Sagittarius axis, it is always important that relationships hold the potential for continued growth, development and exploration. For so long as there is more to be discovered from the other, or the relationship itself is one of continual discovery, all will be well. But if a relationship becomes static or, worse still, restrictive, there will usually be a need to establish distance and to move on.

Gemini/Sagittarius: The Axis of Exploration

Developmental theory identifies an important stage around the age of a year or so, when the child develops the impulse and the ability to start exploring, walking and talking, and is physically capable of moving out of his mother's orbit. If the child is going to learn to stand on his own feet and thrive in the wider world, he needs to develop self-confidence and self-agency. At an age when he is still completely dependent on the other for his survival, it is an act of daring and excitement to strike out on his own, and there is a natural compulsion to do so. Research shows that the child will constantly look to his carer/s for signals either of reassurance or fear – to discover whether his adventurous moves are safe or dangerous.

If the mother is sufficiently confident and secure in herself, she will share or encourage the child's growing sense of adventure, while paying adequate attention to his physical safety. He will be encouraged to explore his surroundings, to enjoy his independence and autonomy, and to develop his own personal interests, tastes and preferences, learning ever more about himself and the world around him. Adequately supported, he can pass through this delicate transitional stage without any difficulty.

The Owned/Disowned Child – and the Symbiotic Character Style

It is believed that the *symbiotic character style* is originally constructed as a defensive adaptation caused by the mismanagement of the child's natural impulse and ability to explore his ever-expanding surroundings.

The parent/s or carer/s may be afraid of, or threatened by, the natural development of the child's self-agency. His first steps towards initiative and adventure may be discouraged or, to the extent that they are inconvenient or dangerous, punished. With over-protective, or 'helicopter parenting', the child's natural drive towards self-discovery and independence are compromised. Equally, the circle drawn by the parents may simply be too small or limited to contain the mental and physical energy, excitement and enthusiasm of the Gemini/Sagittarius child.

Star Crossed: Astrology, Personality Theory and the Meeting of Opposites

He may find himself in a double bind, caught between a fear of abandonment or punishment, if he dares to move beyond the boundaries deemed safe by his carers, and a fear of entrapment, if he stays within them. Instinctively he wishes to escape the confines of the system he is born into, but fears the punishment and feelings of guilt if he does so. In order to avoid re-experiencing this inner conflict, he may adopt one or both of the following defensive adaptations, identifying as either the **Owned** or **Disowned** child. As always, the greater the conscious emphasis on one end of the spectrum becomes, the greater the unconscious, autonomous, drive of the opposite pole also becomes.

The withdrawal of support or approval by the parent/s can be particularly terrifying for a child at this stage, and his emotional reaction is **panic.** The 'owned child' adapts by curtailing his sense of adventure and growing independence and learns to restrain himself. He blocks the development of his own beliefs, opinions and actions and adopts a compromised false dependency and enmeshment, which is approved by the family's value systems. One of the most recognisable traits on this axis is the feeling of guilt associated with independent action. Right into adulthood, he still expects to be punished for transgressing parental or socially approved boundaries. The 'owned child' absorbs, adopts and perpetuates the beliefs and value systems of the family and culture into which he has been born. Right into adulthood, religious, philosophical, political or legal structures may swallowed whole, often without question. The symbiotically adapted child has learned to look for his identity not in himself but through the incorporation of external values, social systems and structures. Any personal values or views remain unknown and undeveloped.

Conversely, an absence of sufficient parental containment means that no safe perimeter has been drawn from which the child can safely strike out on his own. The uncontained, or disowned, child has no safe internal space to come home to, and therefore no opportunity to discover or explore his own inner world. With no opportunity to build his internal resources, to construct a safe and protected personal space, he remains unknown to himself. It is not surprising, therefore, that he is prone to feeling overwhelmed by the actual or presumed demands of others. Believing, usually unconsciously, that he will be crowded, invaded, restricted or punished if he allows others to get too close, he learns to keep his distance in relationships. Once connections have been made and fully explored, it is not unusual for people on this axis to transfer their attention to new ideas or people.

The disowned child cannot seem to get enough space and easily feels smothered. He develops a premature independence, keeping people at arm's length and refusing to allow anyone to get too close. A pattern of avoiding or running away from commitments and human attachments, known as a fear of engulfment, becomes established.

And yet, the double-bind of this adaptation is that the disowned child has difficulty with separation since, without the opportunity to develop his own inner resources, he remains dependent on others for his identity, which is derived from external objects or other people. The disowned child therefore invests his time and attention in constant involvement with others and with the outer world, with learning or travelling or external activities of one sort or another. But all this activity can be a way of avoiding the fear of standing still and having no alternative but to look within.

Strong attachments are often formed with external objects which represent the safety, consistency and support which was lacking in his early environment. Known as transitional objects, or 'comfort blankets', they act as substitutes to compensate for the absence of primal parental containment. On the Gemini/Sagittarius axis, strong attachments can be made to teachers and mentors, books, systems of thought, philosophies or religions, which come to represent safety and provide a sense of orientation, substitutes for self-knowledge and a sense of personal identity. It is not until he has stopped running away from himself that he can break down his sense of separateness and self-alienation.

The disowned child will be consciously drawn to others who he believes will never engulf, entrap or devour him. But he is unconsciously attracted to people or to situations in which the pattern of engulfment is repeated and from which he will once again feel the need to escape. Extended periods of togetherness or commitment cause anxiety. He cannot seem to get enough space and may interpret any expectations or demands on him as smothering or obligating, and therefore insist on being in control and making all the decisions. If this behaviour becomes extreme, he will be prone to feelings of panic. Anger can be used as a defence mechanism, and he may become hostile or pick fights in order to re-establish distance.

Gemini/Sagittarius Polarisation

The defensive adaptations of the **owned** and **disowned** child belong to the same axis, and, as always, the poles of this axis complement and complete each other. The double bind on this axis is the fear of freedom versus the fear of being trapped. Freedom is often accompanied by guilt and a fear of retribution and, in the case of Sagittarius, a fear of being punished by the gods or by fate. But for Gemini there is an equal fear of being trapped, of not being able to breathe. If the Gemini/Sagittarius axis becomes split, each pole will gradually become more extreme. The unconscious, or disidentified pole, will increasingly take on a life of its own and find autonomous expression.

Gemini finds his identity and meaning through communication. Language is his primary vehicle and his medium is all kinds of information, books and studies, and increasingly social media, which is an ideal platform for connecting with others and sharing ideas. But this can develop to the point where there is no sphere of life which is not almost continually involved with others.

Geminis typically do not have a well-developed sense of their own tastes or preferences, since their likes and dislikes have been adopted rather than developed from within.[1] Ever youthful and inquisitive, and often perpetual students, they prefer to remain uncommitted and unaccountable, reluctant to be pinned down. There are always other viewpoints, angles and perspectives to be considered. The most important thing is not to become trapped, and so it is safer to remain ambivalent, rather than to be held to fixed positions which, like the primal experience of curtailment and restriction, generates feelings of panic.

Cut off from the broader vision and quest for meaning of the Sagittarius pole, the shadow expression of Gemini may emerge. They may become increasingly scattered, restless and evasive. Taken to extremes, they may no longer be able to see the value or purpose of all the information and knowledge they are gathering. They may become increasingly critical or cynical, feeling that everything is ultimately trivial, superficial and meaningless, even to the point of nihilism. The problem is that, ultimately, nothing has meaning unless and until it can be measured against our own values and beliefs.

The Jupiter ruled sign of Sagittarius is larger than life. Cut off from the objectivity, detachment, playful duality and paradoxical world of the Gemini pole, planets in Sagittarius lack a sense of humour. They describe how and where we can come to believe that we have privileged access to the one truth, and therefore feel entitled to impose this on others. Jupiter and planets in Sagittarius or the ninth house, are prone to fundamentalism. They describe how and where we 'play god', with a conviction of always being in the know. Sagittarius is instinctively evangelical, reluctant to accommodate the relative truths of the Gemini pole.

Unable to incorporate, and therefore live by, what they know or believe, Sagittarians may become experts in their field, without making any use of what they know in their own lives, choosing instead to teach or preach it. Natural teachers, they may, in extreme cases, gather students, acolytes or disciples around them, people who will admire and follow them unquestioningly. Paradoxically, they may become increasingly dependent on their followers to bolster their own sense of identity and self-worth.

In personality theory, the therapeutic task for people for whom this axis has become radically split, is to discover their own personal tastes, interests and preferences, and in coming to know and trust themselves, to develop the courage and confidence to voice their own personal and subjective thoughts, opinions and beliefs.

Gemini/Sagittarius Stories

Stories on the Gemini/Sagittarius axis describe the fascination of the unknown. They explore the mutual and often passionate attraction between people of different generational, racial, religious, social or educational backgrounds. Both parties feel they have something to learn from the other, and seek to absorb and incorporate those qualities for themselves. The intellectual, philosophical or spiritual nature of the relationship is ultimately more important than the physical attraction.

Relationships on this axis tend to transgress accepted and approved parental, social or cultural boundaries. But there is a strong desire to explore, expand and extend one's horizons through association with others. Typically, these transgressions generate feelings of guilt and a conviction that they will be punished. There is almost always a severe price to pay for daring to go beyond the safe perimeter drawn by their parent/s or culture. The main characters in the story tend to suffer isolation or alienation from the world they knew before, but they have been radically changed by their experiences, and there is no going back.

Many of the stories which belong to this axis tell of the mutual attraction between a student and a teacher, or mentor and protégé, often with a significant age difference. In these stories, the pupil (usually female) is an ambitious and independent spirit who becomes attracted to a mentor (usually male) with the knowledge or life experience to help them develop their innate but unexplored talent and potential. The pupil is also motivated to gain the recognition and respect of the mentor, and it is all too easy for the pupil to fall in love with a mentor who recognises their potential.

The admired mentor is usually more worldly, cultivated and perhaps world-weary, and is naturally drawn to the pupil, whose adoration makes him feel stronger and more potent, boosts his self-esteem, and breathes new life into him. Ultimately, his attachment is to the admiration of the pupil, and to the renewed inspiration he or she provides for the development of his own work, rather than to the pupil him or herself, whom he uses for his own purposes.[2]

This type of story usually has the hallmark of competition and rivalry. The student desires to extract for her own growth everything her mentor has to offer. Her attachment is ultimately to what she can learn from the mentor rather than to the mentor himself, although this is not normally clear to either party at the beginning. Once the student has achieved her goals and absorbed everything she needs to learn, she will move on to the next person who offers, or appears to offer, new horizons and possibilities.

Normally, the student eventually outgrows or 'sees through' her mentor, and most of these stories end in separation: the couple fall in love, learn all they can from each other and then move on. The secret of success for this kind of relationship is for it to evolve into an equal partnership. The challenge for the mentor is to appreciate the pupil's qualities independent of himself, to tolerate her growing independence and to take her seriously as an equal. The sinister side of this relationship pattern is where the student becomes increasingly diminished as the mentor/teacher swallows up and incorporates for himself the brightness, potential and talent of his protégé – a not uncommon theme on this axis.[3]

As one person in the relationship continues to expand in confidence and gain recognition, the other is subsumed and increasingly diminished, as their vital contribution to the success and stability of the system remains unacknowledged or ignored.

Star Crossed: Astrology, Personality Theory and the Meeting of Opposites

Abelard and Heloise

The tragic relationship between Abelard and Heloise is one of history's most enduring love stories, and one which has all the hallmarks of the Gemini/Sagittarius axis. The story is set in twelfth century Paris and tells of the forbidden love between the brilliant theologian and philosopher Abelard, and his student Heloise, twenty years his junior. It tells of the passionate meeting of their minds, bodies and souls, as both step beyond the accepted social and

Figure 6 Abelard and Heloise
Eleanor Fortescue-Brickdale
(1872-1945)

ethical boundaries of their time, and how they suffer the resulting guilt, punishment and eventual separation.

Their illicit relationship was discovered by Heloise's uncle, Canon Fulbert of Notre Dame, with whom she was staying while she pursued her studies, learning all she could from Abelard, who was her tutor. When their relationship came to light, it scandalized the community in which they lived, and Abelard was punished, brutally attacked and castrated. Heloise, who by this time was pregnant, had to flee for her safety into a convent and give up her child when he was born. Both Abelard and Heloise took holy orders and from that time on they lived in separate monasteries. But their love endured and they continued to write to each other for over twenty years. Their letters survive, and their love for one another is evident throughout, as they promised to remain 'Forever One'. Before the end of his life Abelard wrote: "If I am remembered, it will be for this: that I was loved by Heloise." He died in 1142 at the age of sixty-three, and when

Heloise died twenty years later she was buried beside him. Their bones were moved more than once but, six hundred years later, in 1817, Josephine Bonaparte was so moved by their story that she ordered their remains to be entombed together at the Père Lachaise Cemetery in Paris. To this day, lovers or lovelorn singles from all over the world visit their tomb and leave letters at the crypt, in tribute to the couple or in the hope of finding true love.

Camille Claudel

Camille Claudel's chart has a strong Sagittarius/Gemini emphasis, with Sun conjunct Jupiter in Sagittarius opposite Mars in Gemini. Chiron in Pisces forms a T-square to this opposition.

Camille was a talented sculptor, best known for her passionate, and ultimately self-destructive, relationship with the famous sculptor Auguste Rodin. Her story has inspired several films, plays, a musical and a ballet.

Figure 7 Portrait of Camille Claudel, aged 20 years

Camille was the eldest of three children, raised in an intense and intellectually ambitious family. Her father was particularly attentive to the education of his children and, although Camille had little formal education, she read widely from his well-stocked library.

From a young age, Camille was fascinated by natural materials, particularly stone, and by her teenage years she was already demonstrating a remarkable gift for sculpture. Her precocious talent brought her parents into conflict, since her mother was never able to accept that Camille should

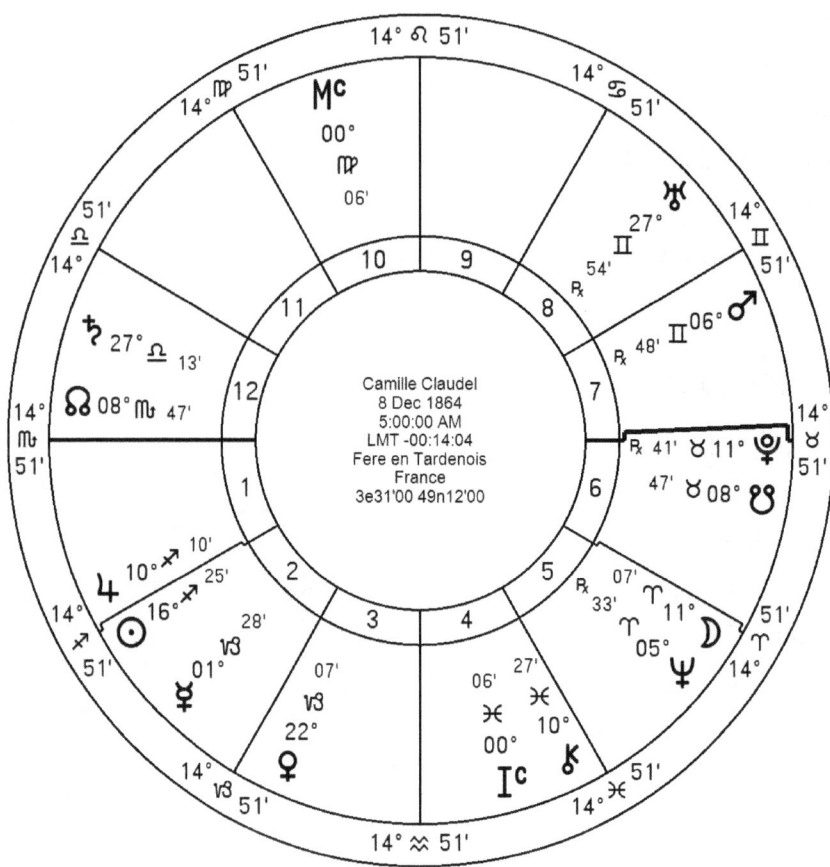

pursue a career rather than get married, the normal expectation for a young woman in the late 19th century.

When Camille was 17 years old, her father moved his family to Paris, to enable his son Paul to pursue his higher education, and so that Camille could take sculpting lessons at one of the few academies open to female students. It was there that she met the sculptor Auguste Rodin, who became her teacher and supervisor. From the outset, Rodin recognised Camille's exceptional talent, but he was also attracted to her fiery and passionate nature, and they fell in love almost immediately. Their passionate, stormy and complicated love story has inspired many interpretations, but it is clear that their artistic alliance inspired both artists and proved to be a decisive turning point in both their lives. Camille had met a teacher who could help her to realise her potential. She became Rodin's muse and model for many of his figures, but she was also his confidante and collaborator, assisting him with commissions as well as creating her own works. For her part, Camille was a source of inspiration for Rodin, and reawakened his artistic energy and vision. Their mutual attraction is clear from the synastry,[4] although knowledge of the affair distressed Camille's family, especially her mother, who had never supported her involvement in the arts.

Rodin procured an apartment for Camille and rented a studio where they could work alone together. The next seven years were a period of happiness and shared passion, one of the most joyous and creative periods of Rodin's artistic life, during which Camille continued to develop her own artistic style.

But Camille became increasingly distressed and enraged that Rodin refused to leave his lifelong companion, Rose Beuret, with whom he lived and with whom he had a son. After an abortion in 1892, when Camille was 28 years old, they began to grow apart, both romantically and professionally. It was important for Camille to establish her artistic independence from Rodin and she wanted to distance herself from him in order to prove he had no hand in the creation of her works.

In 1898, at the age of thirty four, Camille broke off once and for all with Rodin and rented a studio and lodgings in the Ile Saint-Louis where she lived and continued to develop her own style, working ceaselessly and becoming increasingly isolated. At her first exhibition, in 1905, Camille displayed eleven important bronzes. She continued to exhibit at recognized salons and galleries, but found it difficult to get the funding she needed to realise her ideas, although it seems that Rodin continued discreetly to support her, both financially and within the art world.

Nevertheless, Camille became obsessed with Rodin's injustice to her and began to feel persecuted by him and his 'gang'. She was convinced that Rodin was stealing her ideas and that members of the sculpting establishment were conspiring against her. Her feelings of persecution came to dominate her life. She began to have violent outbursts and, in moments of extreme anguish, would destroy every piece of work in her studio. As she became increasingly reclusive, so her physical and mental health diminished. She abandoned her artistic work, and lived in squalor and severe self-neglect.

Camille's father had always been her greatest supporter and protector, but eight days after his death in 1913, on her younger brother Paul's initiative, she was admitted to a psychiatric hospital after suffering an alleged nervous breakdown. Camille was 48 years old and the following year she was transferred to an asylum. The staff regularly proposed to her family that Camille be released, but her mother, who never forgave her for her supposed immorality, refused each time. Camille remained in the asylum until her death in 1943, 30 years later, and was buried there in the communal grave.

Figure 8 Camille Claudel
The Abandonment

Notes

1 The romantic comedy, *Runaway Bride*, starring Julia Roberts and Richard Gere is a good example of this genre.

2 This Gemini/Sagittarius storyline continues to be reframed and reworked in countless different versions. One of the best examples is the film *Educating Rita*, starring Michael Caine and Julie Walters. Films such as *My Fair Lady*, *The King and I* (or Anna and the King), *Crocodile Dundee*, *Legally Blonde*, *The Last of the Mohicans*, *Titanic*, *Moulin Rouge* and *Madame Butterfly* (retold in the musical *Miss Saigon*), tell of the strong attraction between people from different cultures and social backgrounds, and of the price which must be paid for venturing

outside what is deemed to be conventional, socially acceptable behaviour. The punishment, or price to pay for pursuing such relationships, is expulsion from the original symbiotic system, and the resulting isolation. But the cost of remaining within the system can be even higher. The film *Revolutionary Road*, starring Leonardo de Caprio and Kate Winslet, is one chilling example.

3 See, for example, the 2010 film *Tamara Drewe*, and the relationship between Nicholas Hardiment (Roger Allum) and his wife, Beth (Tamsin Greig). Also, the 2017 film *The Wife*, starring Glenn Close and Jonathan Pryce, based on the novel of the same name.

4 Rodin also has a strong Gemini/Sagittarius axis, with a Mercury/Venus/Saturn stellium on Camille's Sun Jupiter conjunction, and his Moon on her 8th house Uranus in Gemini. But there is also a powerful and passionate Taurus/Scorpio theme here, with Camille's Scorpio Ascendant picking up Rodin's Sun-Midheaven-Jupiter stellium. It is clear to see that Camille stimulated, intensified and enhanced his ambitions and his career. In addition, there is a Cancer/Capricorn theme, with Camille's Venus in Capricorn tightly conjunct Rodin's ASC, but opposing his Chiron DES. Rodin was clearly a father figure for Camille, but he always refused to end his long term relationship with Rose Beuret, with whom he lived.

It is significant that Rodin has the same MC/IC axis as Picasso, and therefore may well have had a similar oral character adaptation. In the light of Rodin's Sun/Jupiter/MC conjunction in Scorpio, conjunct Camille's Venus, was Camille right to believe that he possessed and devoured both her and her creativity? Camille was diagnosed as delusional, suffering from paranoid schizophrenia, but her determination to escape his influence, no matter what the cost, may have been an act of great courage, in an era when 'troublesome' women were easily disposed of.

Star Crossed: Astrology, Personality Theory and the Meeting of Opposites

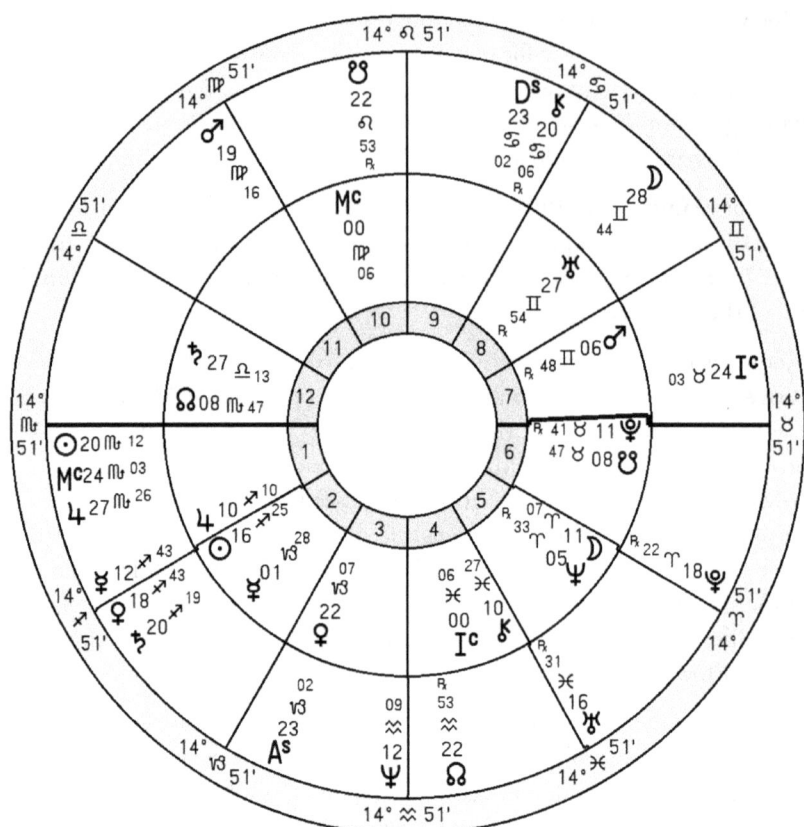

Camille Claudel and Auguste Rodin Bi-wheel

Chapter 7

Leo/Aquarius: The Axis of Identity

The Leo/Aquarius Axis is ruled by the Sun and Saturn (Uranus). As such, it describes the relationship between the unique and creative potential of the child (Sun) and the roles, duties and responsibilities of the adult (Saturn/Uranus). The tension across this axis concerns the balance between subjectivity and objectivity, the individual and the collective, autocracy and democracy, egocentrism and altruism, personal good and the common good. And the question is, to what extent can we be authentically loyal to ourselves (Sun), regardless of what other people think, and to what extent are we influenced by the collective rules, opinions and values of others, either through strict adherence (Saturn) or radical rebellion (Uranus)? The goal is to find ourselves in the crowd.

In personality theory, the initial period of *self and other development* occurs between the ages of one and three. At this stage, the child needs enough safe, interpersonal space within which he can explore the world around him and learn to play on his own, discover what he is capable of and receive adequate and accurate mirroring of his achievements. If his carers can recognise and accommodate his healthy and natural narcissism, the child can learn to enjoy and celebrate his own developing competence and resilience. Taking pride in his accomplishments and achievements, he develops genuine self-esteem, while remaining aware of and responsive to the needs of others.

All being well, and with adequate support and mirroring, the child will pass easily through this developmental stage. With a well-balanced Leo/Aquarius axis we develop self-confidence, the all-important ability to play, and the ability to be generous-spirited, principled, loyal and truthful. With an authentic and genuine self-acceptance, we can be realistic enough to acknowledge our own limitations and therefore to accept the limitations of others. Trusting our own judgement, we can hold our own when necessary, knowing that our contribution is of value, and at the same time we can be magnanimous and authentic in our dealings with others. With an integrated Leo/Aquarius axis, we are confident that our individual contributions have their place in the broader scheme of things, and do not feel compelled either to take over, disrupt or alienate ourselves from the groups or other collectives to which we belong.

The Used Child – and the Narcissistic Character Style

The narcissistic character style is believed to be formed when the normal transitional phase of childish grandiosity is inadequately managed. The parent/s may somehow feel threatened by the genuinely remarkable achievements of the developing child and either ignore or refuse to support, appreciate or encourage his growing self-confidence. This occurs at a stage when the child is particularly sensitive to criticism and humiliation.

The child may instead be used to mirror, aggrandize or fulfil the ambitions and ideals of the parent/s, in which case his real uniqueness and vulnerability are ignored. Instead, he is subjected to 'conditional love', praised and shown off if he lives up to the parent/s' expectations and demands, and ignored, humiliated or punished if he fails to do so. This leads the child to internalise the message: 'Don't be who you are, be who I need you to be and then I will love you'. Such children are *used* rather than generously and authentically supported by their parent/s. Alternatively, the child may be overvalued and overindulged, receiving excessive praise and admiration which is never balanced with realistic feedback. Either way, the child learns that he is not good enough just as he is and must 'perform' when required to do so, living up to some kind of false ideal in order to gain his parent/s' love and approval.

The result can be a deep injury to the development of the child's genuine **self-esteem**. The child who has been used, manipulated and humiliated necessarily lacks self-confidence, and is afraid to actually test himself in the world for fear of failure and further humiliation.

A common defensive adaptation is narcissism, an extreme expression of self-centredness, and the opposite of genuine self-esteem. Puffing himself up, he denies his helplessness and need for support. A typical narcissistic defence is entitlement, the need for excessive admiration, attention and affirmation to bolster his sense of uniqueness and specialness. He exaggerates his talents and achievements, and becomes preoccupied with issues of power and prestige, expecting to be recognized as special, superior and deserving of special treatment without actually having to prove or achieve anything. He demands to be the centre of attention, only interested in events or gatherings which put him in the limelight, and refusing to be involved with, or even sabotaging, group endeavours which do not revolve around him. With exaggerated expectations, and an underestimation of difficulties, he insists that the world owes him a living and that the rules apply to everyone else but not to him.

Grandiosity masks underlying feelings of worthlessness, and he will often make a point of associating only with special, unique or high-status people or organisations, thereby gaining prestige by association. He can be recognised by his interest in social climbing and by his tendency to name-drop.

Another defence is over-achievement, to mask the terror of under-achieving. This is one of the most admired and socially acceptable personality adaptations. People with this character style are often ambitious and extremely successful, charismatic and popular. But they are usually unable to take any real pleasure in their accomplishments and achievements, haunted by the 'imposter syndrome', waiting to be found out. They almost always become their own worst enemies, prone to self-sabotage, unable or unwilling to really test themselves by developing and executing long term plans and goals.

Their pride is easily wounded and they tend to feel deeply humiliated, rejected and threatened when criticised, contradicted or confronted. To protect themselves from re-experiencing the original humiliation or rejection, buried and suppressed underlying feelings of **impotent fury** are unleashed, and they will often react to any slight criticism, real or imagined, with petulance, disdain, rage and/or defiance.

It is safer to find excuses or to blame others than to strive for genuine personal success and achievement, which might lead to failure and humiliation. Psychosomatic illnesses or hypochondria can provide excuses which protect them from facing the realisation of their unfulfilled potential.

Internalising the way they have been treated, they objectify and devalue others as they objectify and devalue themselves. Lacking genuine empathy, they use superficial charm to exploit and manipulate other people in the ruthless pursuit of their own ends. People are initially attracted to their charisma but end up themselves feeling used. There can be a lack of remorse and a cold hard brutality at the core of this personality type which, in its extreme form, is linked to psychopathy.[1]

Leo/Aquarius polarisation

Disturbances on any of the axes occurs if the polarisation becomes extreme, and we consciously identify with only one end of the spectrum and dis-identify with the other. In the case of radical Leo/Aquarius polarisation, the head and heart lose touch with each other and the axis becomes self-defeating.

If we identify with the collective moral and social values of Aquarius, the thinking ego gains the upper hand and we become thought-centred.

Ego development is a normal and necessary stage but, with the birth of objectivity, we learn to stand outside ourselves, which can become a major cause of self-alienation. The heroic 'false self' or 'ego ideal' is constellated as a primitive form of self-sufficiency. With this structure in place, underlying feelings of worthlessness are pushed firmly into the unconscious and, no matter how significant our outer achievements may be, we feel at variance with ourselves. Spontaneous, exceptionally talented, creative and free-spirited people are seen as a threat, and often simultaneously envied, judged and sabotaged. It is psychologically true that groups or collectives tend to ridicule, humiliate or scapegoat individuals who dare to stand out from the crowd.

Aquarius is itself a sign of paradox, since its ruling planets have radically opposed motivations. The Saturn ruler of Aquarius conforms to, and perpetuates, the collective thinking which lies at the root of what is considered to be socially and politically acceptable. The Uranus ruler of Aquarius rebels against these norms, but is just as caught by them. In both cases the unconscious Leo shadow makes an autonomous appearance, which is why planets in Aquarius are often autocratic and deliberately contrary.

If we identify solely with the Leo end of this axis, then we refuse to grow up and insist on remaining entitled and self-centred, demanding special attention and recognition without having to earn it. Difficulties with authority figures are common. The Aquarius shadow is constellated, and we become increasingly sensitive to the opinions and judgements of others. We feel misunderstood and become petulant, belligerent and obstructive, which masks our feelings of inadequacy and lack of genuine self-esteem.

Leo/Aquarius Stories, Myths and Films

There are two main storylines which explore the polarisation and potential for integration on the Leo/Aquarius axis. Both storylines begin with rejection in childhood, and there is almost always a demanding, cold or absent parent who has made the main character feel unworthy of love. In both cases, the main character embarks on a long road of self-discovery, and eventually discovers – or fails to discover – his authentic self, his innate and unique talents and gifts, which he can then share with the world.

The first storyline is a love theme, telling of the loss and recovery of the heart. One leading character, usually male, plays, often very successfully, the heroic 'false self', a role which has been defined for him by his family or by cultural expectations. He may have inherited wealth, power and influence, and find himself effectively trapped in a role which has been chosen for him by his family. Or his worldly success may have brought him to an important or high-status position. Overly responsible and often addicted to work, playfulness and joy are banished from his life, and his behaviour can become arrogant and intimidating, cold and dismissive.

The other leading figure, usually female, tends to be generous hearted, playful and feisty, but, for a variety of reasons, lacks social standing or the right connections, and is unable or unwilling to make her way in the world. But he is attracted to her authenticity, independence, natural liveliness, heart energy and child-like spontaneity. Equally, she is attracted to his worldly power and status, which initially appears to put him out of her reach. For his part, he initially discounts her because of the social obstacles to their union.

But as he grows to recognise her value, his heart opens and he falls in love, discovering for the first time that he can make his own choices, regardless of the expectations, opinions and judgements of others. For her part, she discovers the unique qualities, sensitivity and kindness which lie behind his intimidating persona, and their union enables her to take her place in the world where she feels she belongs. Relevant stories on this axis concern the struggle between these polarised opposites and the transformation which occurs as both parties learn to appreciate, love and value what the other has to offer.[2]

The second storyline on the Leo/Aquarius axis traces the archetypal journey of the hero. Hero myths are particularly relevant on this axis of identity.

They tell of an inner struggle which eventually leads, through a series of trials and difficulties, to the integration of this polarity within the individual. The main character has some sort of unique quality, skill or ability which is vitally important to the fate of a people, group or nation. But, as in the case of many heroes in Greek myth, such as Jason and Perseus, their birth represents a threat to the parents, usually the father, and their birth right is denied to them. They grow up literally not knowing who they are, and exist in a state of naive hubris, or narcissism, as in the Greek myths of Phaeton and Icarus. But their arrogance and lack of self-knowledge leads inevitably to a tragedy, to an event which triggers feelings of guilt, shame, remorse and a period of deep self-questioning. Gradually, as the hero matures, he comes to discover his true and authentic identity, his inner strength and courage, and is ready to grow beyond the defensive 'false self' adaptation which, not knowing himself, he has previously hidden behind. He is finally ready to fulfil his unique destiny, assume his birth-right and share his newly discovered knowledge, skills or abilities with others, thus saving them from harm.[3]

The Story of the Fisher King, Parsifal and the Grail Myth

The story of the Fisher King is a powerful and enduring example of the challenges and potential resolution of the conflicts which exist on the Leo/Aquarius axis. It first appeared in the late twelfth century in *Perceval, the Story of the Grail* by Chretien de Troyes, and there have been many versions of this myth since then, not least in Richard Wagner's famous opera 'Parsifal'.[4]

In Arthurian legend, the Fisher King is the last in a long line of kings charged with keeping the Holy Grail, the miraculous fountain of eternal life. But he had been wounded in the groin, and his impotence had affected the fertility of the entire land, reducing it to a barren wasteland. Everyone in the Grail castle knew about the prophecy that the Fisher King, and therefore the entire kingdom, could only be healed through the actions of an innocent fool, who would spontaneously ask a specific question. In the meantime, all the Fisher King could do was to fish in a small boat on the river near his castle, and wait.

Figure 9 Parsifal in quest of the holy grail
Ferdinand Leeke (1912)

Parsifal (whose name means 'pure fool'), makes an appearance at this point in the story. He was an innocent young man raised in poverty by his mother, without any direction or schooling, and knowing nothing of his dead father (who had in fact been a knight). One day a group of knights rode through his village and, dazzled by the sight of them, he determined to become a knight himself. He made his way to King Arthur's court, where he was initially ridiculed for his naivety, but there was a legend that a damsel in Arthur's court who had not smiled for years would burst into laughter at the sight of the greatest knight – which she did when she saw the innocent Parsifal. The court immediately held Parsifal in high regard and King Arthur knighted him on the spot.

As Parsifal continued on his travels he encountered a mentor who instructed him in the ways of knighthood and revealed to him the critical question – 'Whom does the Grail serve?' – the answer to which would heal the Grail King's wound. But when he eventually arrived back at the Grail castle, he failed to ask the question, and the next morning the castle had disappeared. Parsifal spent twenty years engaged in a series of adventures and gruelling battles, during which time his innocent arrogance and pride were beaten and humbled and he grew in bitterness and disillusionment, until one day he came upon a forest hermit. At first, the hermit scolded him for his failures – especially for not asking the question when he encountered the Fisher King. But he did, however, give Parsifal directions back to the Grail castle. This time, after his long years of earned experience and humility, and finding himself once again in the midst of a great feast at court, he asked the question and was also able to provide the answer: 'You, My Lord, the Grail King'. The Grail King was immediately healed, the entire court erupted in celebration, and the land returned to fertility.

Emma Rauschenbach

Figure 10 Emma Rauschenbach

Emma Rauschenbach was the daughter of a wealthy Swiss industrialist. She was known to be a pleasant and good-natured girl, nicknamed 'Sunny' by her family. But she also had a spirited and fiery nature and a pronounced sense of her own destiny. Emma was both clever and ambitious, and longed to study the natural sciences at the University of Zurich. But the strict rules of proper Swiss society at the beginning of the twentieth century dictated that, for a woman of Emma's status, her education should be designed to prepare her for marriage to a suitable man.

Engaged to the son of one of her father's wealthy business colleagues, Emma's conventional and predictable life was upended when, six years after

Star Crossed: Astrology, Personality Theory and the Meeting of Opposites

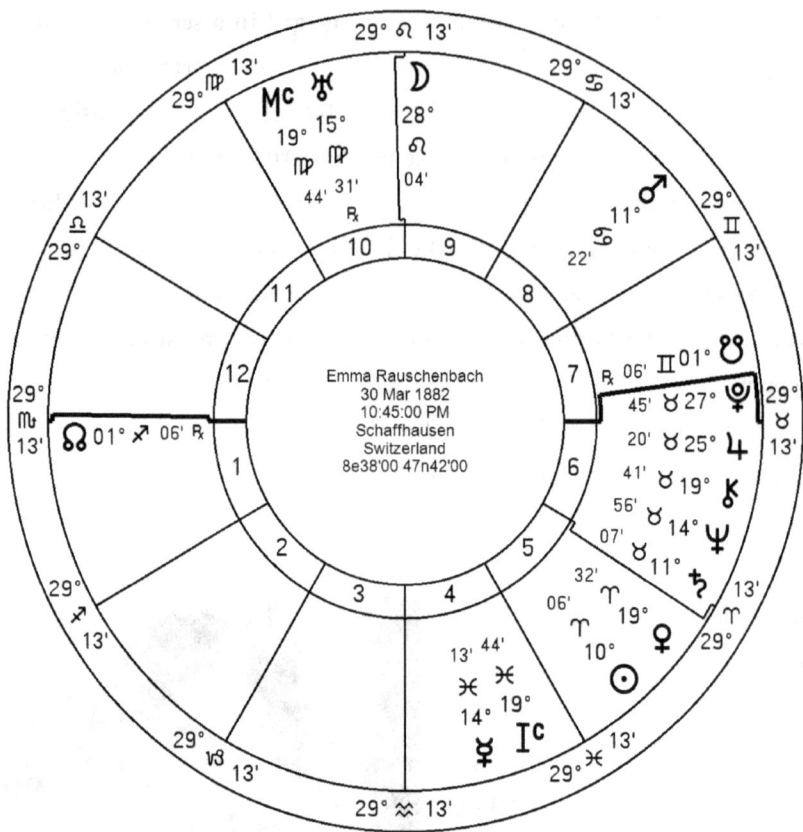

meeting her for the first time, and by now a trained medical doctor, Carl Jung proposed to her. The son of a penniless pastor, Jung dazzled Emma with his intelligence, confidence, and charisma. But more importantly, he offered her freedom from the confines of a traditional haute-bourgeois life. This was Emma's 'call to adventure' and, as is often the case, she initially resisted it, and turned him down. But they were married in February 1903, just before her twenty first birthday. Emma embarked on an unexpected life and found herself challenged to develop in ways that, for a wife and mother of that period, were almost unimaginable.

Right from the start Emma took great interest in her husband's work, participating and collaborating with him. Her family money ensured their financial security, and in the first eleven years of their marriage Emma had five children. In 1908 the family moved to their new home in Kusnacht, on Lake Zurich, and from then on Jung saw private patients at home, gradually developing an international clientele. At the same time he applied himself to his own research work and developed the school of Analytical Psychology. Over the years, with her husband's encouragement, Emma became a noted analyst in her own right, presenting lectures and seminars and becoming a training analyst at the Jungian school in Zurich.

Until recently, very little attention has been paid to Emma's role in the life of her husband, and to her remarkable contribution to the early years of the psychoanalytic movement. Emma's own heroic journey and personal transformation was destined to take place within the crucible of her complex marriage. Emma's Moon and Jung's Sun and DES were in Leo, but Jung's Saturn in Aquarius opposed her Moon. Emma's story sheds further light on relationships with a shared Leo/Aquarius theme.[5]

The Grail legend was of particular significance to Emma Jung, who devoted thirty years of meticulous research to it. Emma died before she could finish her work, but Jung kept his promise to his wife never to talk or write about the Grail Legend, and asked his colleague Marie-Louise von Franz to complete Emma's lifelong endeavour.[i]

Emma believed that, in the context of analytical psychology, the legend was a symbolic representation of the problem of opposites and of the dominant, one-sided masculine values of the collective consciousness. She believed that, like Parcifal, our culture is in thrall to the extraversion of the outer world, and that we are dazzled and distracted, as it were, by the colourful splendour of Arthur's court and its knights. Like Parcifal, we do not take the time to reflect and, like the Grail King, we are cut off from the true source of our inner being, drained and weakened and made sick by our failure to recognise and integrate the shadow. Emma believed that, only by developing the feeling function and taking time to reflect on our

---

i *The Grail Legend, by Emma Jung and Marie-Louise von Franz* 1998, Princeton University Press; New Ed edition.

experiences can we heal the collective imbalance and affect the otherwise uninterrupted and catastrophic chain of outer events.

Like her husband, Emma believed that, ultimately, we serve something far greater than ourselves. But this can only be achieved by the individual. If we are to play our part in healing the collective imbalance, we must first reconcile our personal polarities. The goal of individuation is realised when the ego comes into the service of the greater Self, the Grail, our most authentic nature, our souls.

Emma's biographer, Catrine Clay[ii], describes how exasperating, exhausting and exhilarating it must have been to live with Carl. Jung could be selfish and narcissistic, even something of a bully, and at times his behaviour was close to intolerable. The biographer Aniela Jaffe[iii] wrote that Emma's inner calm beautifully compensated for her husband's often volcanic temper. His undoubted charisma masked a strange and dark interior, and his own heroic journey began in 1913, when he embarked on a critical descent into the unconscious realms of his own being.

But Emma's journey was equally heroic. A remarkably brave and generous woman, she needed all her patience, composure, and powers of common sense, wisdom and maturity – as she attended to the demands of her family, ran a large household, was hostess to Jung's many visitors and actively supported Jung in his work. It seems clear that Jung could never have achieved what he did without Emma's support.

But Emma also has a strong Taurus/Scorpio axis. With Scorpio on her Ascendant, Pluto, the co-ruler of her chart, is conjunct her South Node and Descendant, and part of an intense sixth house stellium in Taurus which includes Jupiter, Chiron, Neptune and Saturn. She struggled with the fact that Jung exerted such power over everyone he met. In particular,

---

ii Catrine Clay (2015) *Labyrinths: Emma Jung, Her Marriage to Carl and the Early Years of Psychoanalysis.*
iii Aniela Jaffe (1983) *C.G.Jung: Word and Image*, Princeton University Press, Bollingen Series.

Leo/Aquarius: The Axis of Identity

it was hard for her to endure his close friendships with two women in particular, which caused serious problems in their marriage. Sabina Spielrein and Toni (Antonia) Wolff were both students and patients of his, and later psychoanalysts in their own right. Toni Wolff was Jung's closest co-worker for several decades, next to his wife, and became the third party in a Jungian ménage à trois. Emma managed to endure his infidelities and to tolerate Toni's presence, but she insisted on her exclusion from all meal times and evenings.

Emma died in 1955, pre-deceasing Jung by almost six years. After her death Jung carved a stone in her name, "She was the foundation of my house". As he grieved for her, he is said to have wailed, "She was a queen! She was a queen!".

Notes

1 There are many successful TV series, such as *Billions* and *Succession*, which follow the ambitious, charismatic and ruthless lives and deeds of psychopathic characters.

2 One popular version of this story is Jane Austen's *Pride and Prejudice*, which continues to spawn many adaptations, such as *Pretty Woman*, *You've Got Mail* and the *Bridget Jones* trilogy. In the *Bridget Jones* films, Mark Darcy (the name of the hero in *Pride and Prejudice*) is a successful and high status international human rights lawyer. He has fulfilled his parents' ambitions for him, but is joyless, stiff and reserved (the Aquarius pole). Bridget Jones is an aspiring journalist, childlike, spontaneous and fun loving (the Leo pole), with a penchant for 'messing up'. Through their association, Darcy's heart is opened and, in a series of developments, including the birth of her baby in the third film, Bridget Jones grows up and becomes successful in her own right. *Jane Eyre* and *Rebecca* are also well known examples of this relationship theme.

In the immensely successful film *Pretty Woman*, the main roles are played by Richard Gere and Julia Roberts. The story tells of the encounter between a wealthy and influential businessman, with all the right social contacts and connections. He has devoted himself to the continued development of the business empire he has inherited from his father, but his personal life is bleak and empty. He meets a woman working as a prostitute who brings him to life and teaches him to live from the heart rather than the head. In the process, she gains the social standing and opportunities she craves.

The gender roles played by the main characters are just as often reversed such as, for example, in the film *Titanic*, one of the most popular, and compulsively watched films of all time. This is the story of Rose (Kate Winslet), a young woman trapped by the expectations of her high-class but debt-ridden family and condemned to make a socially acceptable, but loveless, marriage. Jack Dawson (Leonardo DiCaprio) is an itinerant worker who wins a third-class ticket on the Titanic. Their passionate love affair begins when Rose contemplates throwing herself off the stern of the ship, and Jack rescues her.

The Snow Queen is a fairy tale by the author Hans Christian Andersen. First published in 1845, it has been constantly adapted in various media, including animations and television drama. Most recently the story has been used as the basis for the immensely successful Disney cartoon films *Frozen* and *Frozen II*. These films are particularly powerful examples of the Leo/Aquarius story and their global success is evidence of their archetypal relevance.

The Snow Queen begins with the severing of the Leo/Aquarius axis, the head and the heart. An evil troll makes a magic mirror with the power to distort the appearance of things, making everything look worse than it is. Psychologically, this event describes the loss of the magical world of childhood, as our egos develop and we become estranged from our true natures. When the mirror shatters into billions of pieces, the splinters find their way into people's hearts, freezing them like blocks of ice, and into their eyes so that they can only see the bad and ugly in people and things.

Kay and Gerda were children who lived next door to each other in a large city. They were playmates, devoted to each other, but one day, splinters of the mirror entered Kay's heart and eyes. His personality changed and he became cruel and aggressive, telling Gerda he no longer cared for her. The only beautiful and perfect things to him now were the tiny snowflakes that he could see through a magnifying glass.

The following winter he was fascinated to see the Snow Queen drive through the market square in her white sleigh, as she travelled throughout the world with the snow. When Kay approached her, she abducted him to her ice palace and gardens, in the lands of permafrost, near the North Pole, where she kept him prisoner. She set him a puzzle, and promised to release him from her power if he could form the word "eternity" out of pieces of ice.

Meanwhile, Gerda, who was heartbroken at Kay's disappearance, set off to find him. Eventually, after a series of adventures, she discovered the Snow Queen's palace. Gerda found Kay alone, almost immobile on a frozen lake, which the Snow Queen called the "Mirror of Reason", engaged on the task that the Snow

Queen had given him. Seeing him so trapped, Gerda wept warm tears on him, which dislodged the splinters from his eyes and melted his heart. Kay was saved by the power of Gerda's love.

Leaving the Snow Queen's domain together, they returned to their home town where everything was the same, but they discovered that they had changed. They were now grown up, and delighted to see that it was summertime.

3 Just a few of the immensely popular and successful stories which retell the myth of the archetypal hero are *The Wizard of Oz, Star Wars, Harry Potter, Top Gun, The Lord of the Rings* and *The Hunger Games*.

In the 1986 film *Top Gun*, Tom Cruise plays the character of the hero, the young naval aviator Lieutenant Pete 'Maverick' Mitchell, a young naval aviator who is sent to Top Gun, the naval fighter weapons school. The plot has all the usual components of the archetypal journey of the hero.

His father, who had also been a naval aviator, lost his life in suspicious circumstances, and Maverick is determined to prove himself and to redeem the family name. Immensely talented but arrogant and narcissistic, his reckless and dangerous flying breaks all the rules of engagement. He becomes a rival to top student 'Iceman' Kazansky [the two leading characters represent the ice and fire of the Aquarius/Leo axis], but in a practice engagement he and his flying partner Goose go into an unrecoverable flat spin. Like the Greek myths of Phaeton and Icarus, his arrogance leads him to fall, literally, out of the sky, and Goose is killed.

This tragedy heralds the beginning of Maverick's 'dark sea journey', during which he is overcome by guilt and remorse. He seeks advice from Viper, an older man, who reveals that, contrary to official reports, Maverick's father died heroically. Viper tells Maverick that he can succeed if he can regain his self-confidence. His girlfriend, Charlie, continues to believe in him and challenges him not to give up.

Maverick returns to Top Gun and, in a final crisis situation, he faces his demons and wins through. He and Iceman return from their mission triumphant, with a newfound respect for each other. Maverick has grown and gained maturity and, offered any assignment, he chooses to become an instructor at Top Gun, a role in which he can pass on what he has learned.

Again and again, Tom Cruise plays the role of the hero who is severely tested but emerges transformed and triumphant, able to 'save the world', to right the social wrongs and rescue and redeem the collective. Tom Cruise's birth time is not known, but his nodal axis is Leo/Aquarius, with Saturn exactly on his South Node in Aquarius, and Moon, Venus and Uranus in Leo. Some of his most famous 'hero' roles are in *A Few Good Men* (1992), *The Firm* (1993), *Jerry*

Maguire (1996) and *Jack Reacher* (2012). He also plays the agent Ethan Hunt in the successful six-film series *Mission Impossible* (originally 1996).

Female heroes are increasingly common in films. Jennifer Lawrence, for example, played the starring role as Katniss Everdeen in *The Hunger Games* film series (2012-2015), which established her as the highest-grossing action-heroine of all time. Jennifer has a Leo/Aquarius nodal axis, with Sun and Venus in Leo.

4   Jungian analyst Robert A. Johnson suggests in his book *'He'* that the story of Parsifal and the Grail myth describes the evolution of the psychology of the masculine, in both men and women, and is as relevant now as it has ever been.

5   There is a powerful synastry between Emma and Carl's charts, made all the more prominent by the involvement of both nodal axes. Emma's ASC/DES and nodal axis is tightly conjunct Jung's MC/IC axis. This placement alone suggests Emma's significance in Jung's career and home life. In addition, her Sun in Aries is exactly conjunct Jung's North Node. She must have given him courage to believe in himself. Her emotional strength and commitment to her family are indicated by her eighth house Mars in Cancer, on Jung's Mercury Venus conjunction, and tightly square his nodal axis.

Figure 11 Emma and Carl Jung

Jung was well aware of his many inner contradictions, one of which can be described by his ASC/DES across the Aquarius/Leo axis, and by Saturn, his chart ruler, in Aquarius in the first house and his Sun in Leo in the seventh house.

   On the Aquarius end of this spectrum, he adapted to the conventional world of his time and aimed to achieve a civilized and prestigious lifestyle. He was ambitious for academic success, studied science and trained as a medical doctor. On the Leo end of this spectrum, he had an infectious and hearty love of life and great charisma, although by all accounts he could also be childish and undisciplined. This 'grandiose self' was designed to offset painful feelings of inferiority, anxiety and insecurity.

Leo/Aquarius: The Axis of Identity

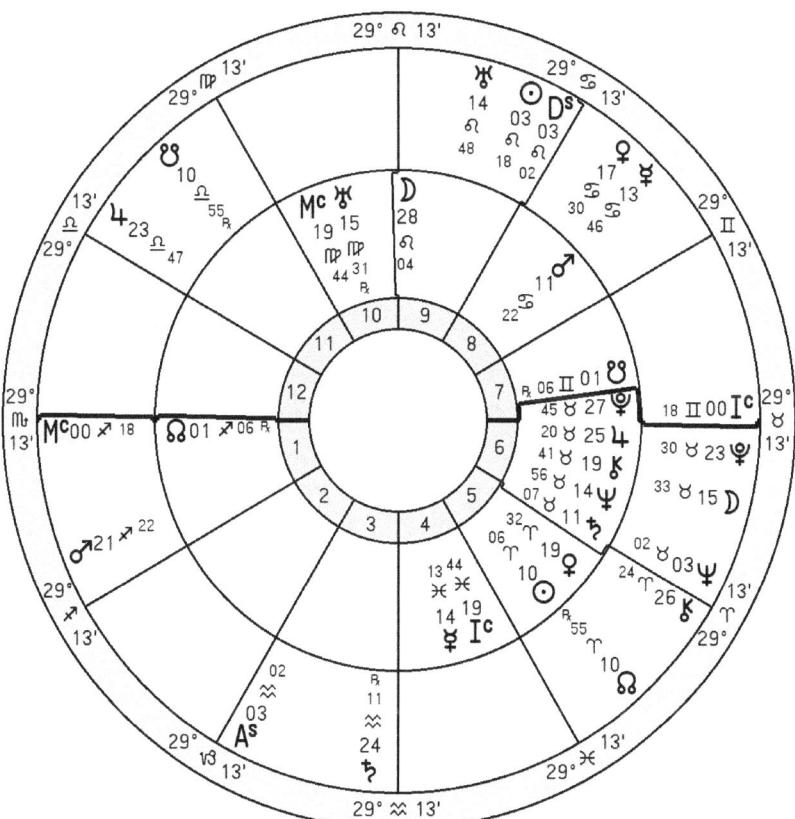

Emma (inner chart) and Carl (outer chart) Jung

89

Chapter 8

Virgo/Pisces: The Axis of Service

The Virgo/Pisces axis is ruled by Mercury and Jupiter (Neptune) and has a natural affinity with the 6th/12th house axis in the birth chart. It concerns the relationship between skilful, practical efficiency, work and service, and the desire to escape from the harsh realities and demands of this world and to inhabit a richly imaginative, dreamlike and boundaryless existence. The goal on this axis is to find a healthy balance between self-definition and self-sufficiency, and the yearning to remain undifferentiated, remain merged with the greater whole, and to go with the flow.

As with all axes, the challenge is to become conscious of both poles and develop the flexibility to dance between them. In balance, this axis is immensely creative and evocative, with the ability to give skilful form and shape to the boundless imagination, in writing, music, dance, film, photography, art and artistic expression generally. In other words, the challenge is to balance the tension between order and chaos, control and trust, and to develop genuine compassion and care, both for ourselves and others. With a sufficiently well-developed sense of personal autonomy and independence comes the ability to say 'no', and the freedom to make choices which are neither evasive, avoidant or sacrificial, nor designed to maintain control at all costs.

The Mercury-ruled earth sign of Virgo is realistic, practical and efficient, discriminating and skilful. Virgo is analytical, self-critical and something of a perfectionist. She is modest, hardworking, and at her best when creating order out of chaos. Her self-esteem grows as she develops the confidence to make her own choices, and when she has work which serves a useful and necessary function. But, with the sign of Pisces at the opposite end of this spectrum, Virgo can all too easily find herself feeling uncomfortably out of control and overwhelmed by the needs and demands of others, which can lead to burn-out or chronic anxiety, and physical symptoms such as digestive problems.

For the mutable water sign of Pisces, the world is a colourful and constantly shifting kaleidoscope of impressions and feelings. Pisces is immersed in her environment, absorbing, reflecting and merging. Everything has its attractions, connections and possibilities. The Jupiter (and Neptune) ruled sign of Pisces is expansive, imaginative, intuitive and inclusive, and absolutely refuses to be defined, limited or controlled. Pisces is chameleon-like, adept at camouflage and prone to hiding behind any number of smokescreens in order to avoid being pinned down or held responsible. With the demands of Virgo at the opposite end of this spectrum, Pisces can employ deception, manipulation and passive-aggression as covert methods of attempting to remain in control.

The Defeated Child – and the Masochistic Character Style

In personality theory, it is believed that the masochistic character structure is originally formed in the crucible of the power struggles of the 'terrible twos', when the child begins to develop a desire for self-determination, and seeks to assert her own will. If the parent/s understand and recognise the importance of this stage, and if they are sufficiently sensitive, secure and confident in themselves, they will be capable of 'picking their battles' and, when it is safe and appropriate, to allow the child to assert her own will and to 'win'. In an optimal environment, the child will develop the confidence to make her own choices and stand on her own feet, while remaining aware of, and sensitive to, the needs of others.

If, however, for whatever reason, the establishment of healthy independence is thwarted, the **defeated child** has no choice but to sacrifice her own development and surrender to the will of the parent/s. The child cannot afford to 'win', since she is dependent on her carer/s for her survival. One or both of two main character styles can develop, known as the **dependent** and **rescuer** adaptations, which, to a greater or lesser extent, are expressions of a Virgo/Pisces axis which has become split or dissociated. These adaptations are not consciously chosen, but rather they serve as workable defence structures constructed in order to try and avoid the anxiety generated by this impossible double bind.

The Dependent Adaptation

A dependent adaptation can develop if the parent/s maintain excessive control and refuse to allow the child to be self-determining. Rebellion, defiance and individual self-expression are punished, and the child, who initially puts up a considerable struggle in the battle of the wills, has no option but to give in and allow the domination, surrendering to the will of the parent. If her will is persistently, intrusively and, in extreme cases, sadistically beaten into submission, a pattern of **self-defeat** becomes established.

In a sense, the child's will has been broken before it ever had a chance to be formed. She adapts by becoming characteristically self-deprecating, self-sacrificing and over-pleasing, which explains why people with dependent adaptations are often popular and much liked. They look to others to take the lead and are not inclined to be demanding or provocative. They are biddable, submissive and obliging, loyal and considerate towards those upon whom they depend, willing to give their all.

Abdicating self-responsibility, they internalize the beliefs and values of significant others. They are inclined to see others as they wish they were rather than as they actually are, sustaining a naïve, idealized and sometimes fictional view of the people upon whom they depend. Overly attentive, accepting and allowing, they take more care of others than of themselves. But what looks like love, affection and devotion can, in fact, be driven by a primal fear of abandonment.

With this adaptation in place, the dependent or co-dependent adult finds it difficult to initiate projects or to do things on her own, not because she lacks the skills, motivation or energy but because she lacks self confidence in her judgment or abilities, and has difficulty disagreeing with others because, above all, she fears the loss of their support or approval. She will even meet unreasonable demands, agree with things she believes are wrong and subordinate her needs to those of others. In extreme cases, she may even tolerate intimidation, abuse and infidelity, settle for sex as proof of love, or be defenseless against predation. The point here is that she feels she has no choice. Her core fear of abandonment leads to submissive behaviour and an excessive need to be taken care of, at any cost. But her attachment figures are basically interchangeable. If a significant dependency is lost, she tends to become quickly and indiscriminately attached to the most readily available other who she believes will never abandon her.

Self-sabotage and passive aggression are recognized aspects of a dependent or co-dependent adaptation.

Self-sabotage is an unconscious act of revenge, a way of trying to get even which carries an element of satisfaction. Known as the masochistic adaptation, the enjoyment of one's own defeat is securely hidden from consciousness and one of the most deniable acts of aggression. The masochist becomes her own worst enemy. Self-defeat and self-punishment become the only safe way for the blocked and now distorted will to find expression. A perverse pleasure is taken in self-induced pain and, once established, is extraordinarily resistant to change. People with masochistic personalities are remarkably stubborn. Their rebellion is disguised, hidden and deniable, and absolutely maddening for anyone who cares about them. Typically, they make others feel responsible for their pain but will reject or render ineffective any attempts to help them.

Abusive relationship patterns can be established as a template, and people with a dependent adaptation can find themselves in humiliating, self-defeating relationships which may well be physically, emotionally and/or mentally abusive. They will be uninterested in, or consistently reject, people who treat them well, and choose people and situations which lead to disappointment, failure or mistreatment, even when better options are clearly available.[1]

Masochists make contact with others by being of service, but usually with a joyless, martyr-like, guilt-inducing quality. They may engage in excessive, unsolicited self-sacrifice on behalf of others, and yet fail to accomplish tasks which are important to them, in spite of their ability to do so. People with this adaptation provide the solid backbone of any number of social organisations, including their own families. Their attitude is one of self-sacrifice, service and forbearance, and the ability to cope with a great deal of frustration. They may always be the one who tries to fix things, walking on eggshells and compromising themselves in order to accommodate the agendas or timing of others. But, while carrying out a life of acceptable and socially-sanctioned roles and obligations, they can be plagued by a kind of chronic stasis and diminished energy. They may, for example, work in the caring professions but seem unable or unwilling to care adequately for themselves.

Chronic anxiety can lead to over-thinking and over-analysis. An excessive preoccupation with details, rules, lists or schedules can obscure the main point of the activity and, if one problem is solved, it is immediately replaced by another problem. Driven by a need to remain in control, an over-conscientious perfectionism interferes with task completion, and is carried out at the expense of flexibility, openness and efficiency, exacerbated by a refusal to delegate tasks or work to others.

Despite having all the necessary social skills, they tend to reject any opportunities for pleasure or leisure activities, and are reluctant to acknowledge enjoying themselves. They may be self-deprecating, and

Virgo/Pisces: The Axis of Service

respond to positive personal success with depression or guilt, while feeling an unconscious envy and disdain for others who seem to enjoy success and even life itself, without seemingly having to work at it.

The ability to endure pain and deprivation is seen as an admirable quality. Long-suffering, self-torturing and self-defeating behaviour seems to suggest a 'need to suffer', or Messiah complex. Deprivation becomes a life style, a noble calling, since to embrace pleasure, success and fulfilment would risk causing the whole defensive structure, including the values that uphold it, to collapse.

Attitudes to money and possessions on this axis are revealing. On one extreme end of this spectrum, financial constraints or limitations are refused or ignored, while on the other extreme end, money is hoarded against imaginary future catastrophes, resulting in an excessively miserly spending style towards both themselves and others. Worthless or worn-out items may continue to be hoarded, even when they have outlived their purpose or function.

Passive aggressive behaviour is also a feature of this character style, a subtle, pervasive and persistent resistance, evasion and obstruction in response to others whom they perceive as more powerful than them. The understandable resentment, anger and frustration are pushed into the unconscious, into the shadow, from where it operates against themselves or against others. Unconscious aggression is expressed so covertly that it is virtually impossible to recognise and confront. The masochist uses passive-aggression to provoke retaliation, enraging, frustrating and alienating those around them. For example, the defeated child may say 'yes', when she really means 'no', and then somehow 'forget' to do what she has agreed to do. This is the only way she feels she can wield power and control over the other, whom she deeply resents.

Passive aggressive people may present themselves as martyrs, using self-pity, physical or mental collapse as excuses, when in fact they are actually engaged in manipulative entrapment. This behaviour not only makes others feel guilty, but also resentful that they are being 'sucked in' to manoeuvres which are not of their making.

A classic adaptation is to be a good girl or boy, to try and get everything right. But under the surface there is often a great deal of unacknowledged resentment which, because it is too dangerous to express overtly, is expressed through spitefulness, hostility and even cruelty towards others.[2]

The Rescuer Adaptation

At the opposite end of this spectrum of the defeated child, the parent/s may have been out of control or profoundly unsafe. They may have been ill or absent, addicts or victims of one sort or another. In such cases, the child feels she has no alternative but to take premature responsibility, and for some people on the Virgo/Pisces axis, rescue and control become the central, life-long, theme in relationships. Rescuers are often attracted to people who are disturbed, ill, vulnerable or needy – anyone, in fact, whom they believe needs rescuing. They may remain unrealistically optimistic in the face of their partner's repeated depressions, violence or betrayals, and may continue to believe, in the face of evidence to the contrary, that they can restore their loved one to health and to their full potential. But what looks like selfless devotion to the other is, in fact, an attempt to repair the helplessness they themselves felt as a child, a displaced attempt to rescue and heal the inadequate or absent parent.

There is a high price to pay for the dependent and rescuer adaptations, both for the 'defeated child' and for those they are in contact with. The child who has had to sacrifice the natural and healthy development of her independence, is unable to establish her own identity, separate from others. But her unconscious rage, resentment and frustration at having to make such a sacrifice continues to operate covertly, from the shadow, against herself and against others.

Virgo/Pisces: The Axis of Service

The invalid and healer, rescued and rescuer, victim and saviour are bound together on this axis. Selfless devotion to a wounded or inadequate partner is typical of the most extreme rescue scenarios, but the underlying motivation may be to maintain control. Rescuers often feel more comfortable in relationships where the other is too weak or ill to leave. Taking on the rescuer role can therefore be a defensive tactic which masks the underlying fear of abandonment. It can also be an act of self-sabotage, a way of avoiding the hard work of breaking old patterns, which can lead to release from the entrapment of dependency on others. One example from my own practice concerns a man with an alcohol dependency and his wife, who identified herself as his carer and rescuer. When the man eventually managed to free himself from this addiction, this threatened the polarised Pisces/Virgo 'system' they had constructed, and the wife's role and identity as a selfless and long-suffering carer. Unable or unwilling to free herself from her collusion in this dissociated system, or to make any changes herself, she began to hide bottles of wine and spirits around the house for him to find.

Health and the Virgo/Pisces Axis

Health issues are always relevant on this axis. Mysterious, debilitating and persistent illnesses, often with no obvious physical cause or cure, can be a feature.[3]

In healthy relationships the energy exchange between two people is mutually enhancing, supportive and sustaining. In unhealthy relationships the energy exchange is addictive, draining and mutually destructive, and so the question is whether a relationship feeds or drains us energetically, and whether we feel we have a choice.

Relationships where a negative symbiosis is formed are analogous to the relationship between a host and a parasite. One person takes on the role of the host, or martyr, endlessly sacrificing herself to the other, and in the process becoming more and more energetically depleted. The parasite feeds off this borrowed energy and, in personality theory, a well-known script for this kind of relationship goes something like this: 'If I stay, I will die; if I leave, you will die'.

All archetypes carry psychic energy, and the archetype of health and wholeness is balanced by the archetype of the invalid, of a chronic state of deficiency.[i] The tyranny of the invalid is a well-known aspect of passive-aggression, and the capacity of an invalid to elicit another's help and sympathy is an example of the power and control of weakness. If these two archetypes become dissociated, or split, the person playing the invalid role can become tyrannical, egotistical and life-denying. Consciously chosen service or devotion to a cause or to another person involves the individual will, and freely made choices do not have the unmistakable 'sticky' feeling of unconscious sacrifice.

Addictions, including an addiction to suffering, are particularly prevalent on this axis, and can become the most powerful dependencies of all. Their function is to help deny or block the understandable rage of the defeated child who has had to sacrifice her self-development. With a passive-aggressive dependent adaptation, addictions can be used as an act of revenge. On the extreme Pisces end of this spectrum, the internalised and usually unconscious motivation is to maintain control by poisoning ourselves before we can be poisoned by others.

Conversely, on the extreme Virgo end of this spectrum, there can be a great fear of accepting or absorbing anything at all from others or from the outside world, which is likely to be seen as poisonous. There can be a refusal to let people become too close, and/or a hypersensitivity to the environment, which may manifest, for example, in a range of debilitating allergies or other physical symptoms. There can also be an obsessive need for cleanliness and/or control over one's environment or body. Body

---

[i] Adulf Guggenbuhl-Craig *From the Wrong Side*, p.146. See also *Power in the Healing Professions*.

Virgo/Pisces: The Axis of Service

control often finds expression in ritualistic, and often extremely harsh, or punishing, diet and exercise regimes.

Virgo Pisces Stories

Stories relevant on this axis concern the exchange of energy between two people or between an individual and an organisation. This exchange can be energising, for example in the case of dedicated service to others, or to one's job, or to a religion or cause. There is almost always a powerful psychic union which, providing that the exchange of energy is equal and consciously chosen, can be immensely creative, supportive and life affirming. Alternatively, it can be draining, exhausting or destructive, in which case the story usually includes the theme of escape.

If the exchange of energy is autonomous, people caught in this kind of system remain locked together, in unconscious mutual collusion, whether for good or ill. Neither party can extract themselves from the system unless, or until, they realise they have a choice. There are many variations of the Virgo/Pisces story, both in fiction and in real life[4].

In symbiotic relationships there can also be identity confusion, or psychic identity theft, insinuation or impersonation, as the energy shapeshifts, passing backwards and forwards between two people.[5]

The archetype of the vampire is a psychological structure we all share, which explains its continuous presence in myth and literature, regardless of cultural variations. Vampire stories are as popular now as they have ever been.[6] Vampires are mythical beings who subsist by feeding on the life essence and vitality (generally in the form of blood) of their victims. Zombies, the living dead or undead, dementors and wraiths all belong to this genre. For a variety of reasons, they have no contact with the wellsprings of life within themselves and must therefore feed off others.

There is a fatal symbiosis, an unconscious psychic connection between the victimizer and victim. The victim has an equal part to play, since they desire, however unconsciously, to be possessed and controlled. The vampire has to be invited in, and returns night after night while his victim visibly weakens. Eventually victims are themselves transformed into vampires, and the pattern begins to repeat itself.

Most psychological interpretations of the vampire legend are Freudian, seeing it as a form of unconscious wish fulfilment, but the psychic vampire is a powerful archetypal pattern which describes the way that people trade energy. Most of us have had the experience of people who charge or subtly drain our energy levels.[7]

Wuthering Heights

Wuthering Heights was written in 1846, and is Emily Bronte's only published novel. The story has inspired many adaptations, in films, radio, television, a ballet, three operas and the 1979 hit song by Kate Bush.

When the book was first published, the vivid sexual passion and power of its language and imagery, and its unusually stark depiction of mental and physical cruelty, impressed, bewildered and appalled reviewers. Dante Gabriel Rossetti referred to it as "a fiend of a book – an incredible monster ... the action is laid in hell". The book went on to become an English literary classic, although Emily Bronte

Figure 12 Wuthering Heights

Virgo/Pisces: The Axis of Service

never knew the extent of the fame her only novel would achieve, since she died at the age of thirty, a year after its publication.

The narrative centres on the overwhelming, and ultimately doomed relationship between Catherine Earnshaw and Heathcliff, an obsessive and unresolved passion which eventually destroys them and the people around them.

The signs are there from the beginning. Cathy has no mother and Heathcliffe is an orphan who has been abandoned by his parents. When Cathy's father brings Heathcliff to live with them, they form a strong bond and declare themselves inseparable for life. Cathy has a shattering revelation of demonic, psychic possession when she cries, "I am Heathcliff!"

Cathy's relationship with Heathcliff conforms to the themes of Gothic romance, in which the woman falls prey to the more or less demonic instincts of her lover, who suffers from the violence of his feelings and is entangled by his thwarted passion. At one stage Heathcliff is described as a vampire, but they are both caught up in this dynamic. Each is psychically possessed by the other.

As Cathy grows up, she distances herself from Heathcliff and, in an act of revenge and self-sabotage, she marries her more socially acceptable neighbour, Edgar Linton. Some critics have identified her as a type of gothic demon, since she shapeshifts in order to marry him, by assuming a domesticity which is contrary to her true nature and destructive to all involved.

The tragedy is that neither Heathcliff nor Cathy have a sense of their own independent identity. Heathcliff's life seems to depend on Cathy, and the romantic rejection is devastating. When Cathy dies in childbirth, the psychic connection remains as strong as ever, and her memory continues to haunt him. Heathcliff's life is reduced to anger and retribution and he embarks on destroying the two families which he believes have ruined his life. His actions are motivated by jealousy and a need for control. Eventually he kills himself in order to be reunited in death with Cathy.

Star Crossed: Astrology, Personality Theory and the Meeting of Opposites

Emily Bronte

Emily Bronte has Scorpio/Taurus ASC/DES, with Mars and Venus, the rulers of her ASC/DES relationship axis, conjunct on the Midheaven in Virgo, and opposite Saturn in Pisces on the IC. The transpersonal ruler of Emily's chart is Pluto, conjunct Chiron, also in Pisces and just into the fifth house, and part of this opposition. The opposition makes a T-Square to the Uranus/Neptune conjunction in Sagittarius in the first house, an outlet which describes the immense power of her imagination. Emily's life vividly reflects many of the themes on the Virgo/Pisces axis.

Figure 13 Emily Bronte

Emily Bronte grew up in Haworth, in the bleak West Riding area of Yorkshire, a land of wild moors, open, grassy areas unsuitable for farming. She had a solitary and reclusive nature, and a great love of nature and animals. Her love of the moors, and of all wild, free creatures, is manifest in *Wuthering Heights*.

Emily was the fifth of six children, and when she was three years old her mother died from cancer. Her father had been a schoolteacher and tutor before becoming an Anglican minister. Emily's three older sisters were sent to the Clergy Daughters' School, where they encountered the abuse and privations later described by Charlotte in *Jane Eyre*.

At the age of six Emily joined her sisters at the school for a brief period, but, after a typhoid epidemic and the death of her sister Maria, she was removed from the school along with Charlotte and Elizabeth, who also died soon after their return home.

Virgo/Pisces: The Axis of Service

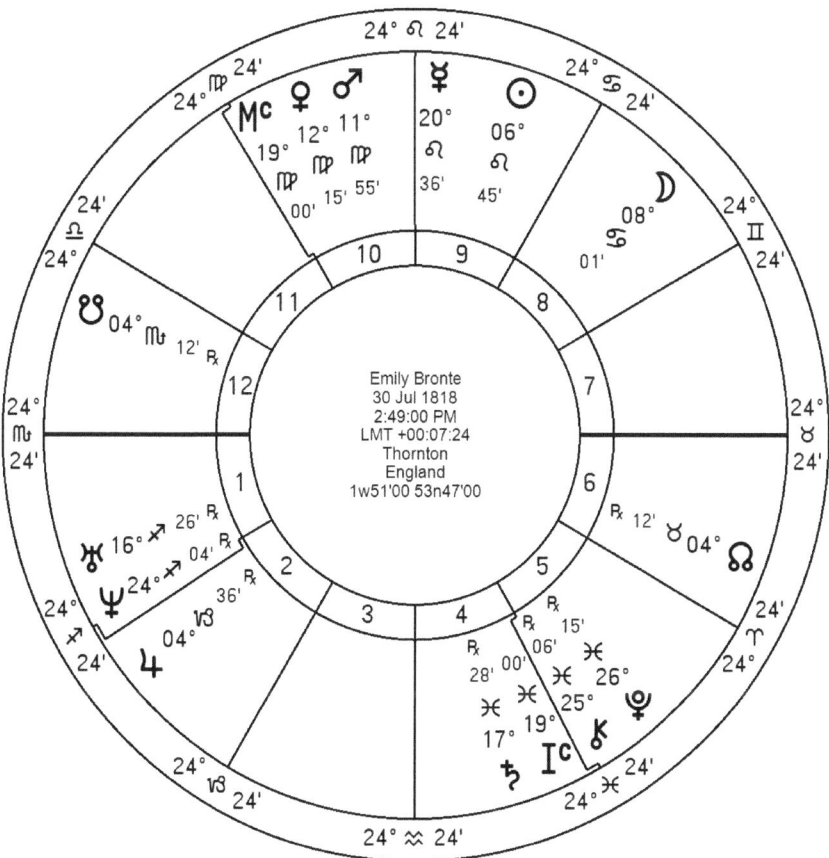

The early death of their mother and two older sisters drew the remaining children close together. The three remaining sisters and their brother, Patrick Branwell, were thereafter educated at home by their aunt, Elizabeth Branwell, their mother's sister, and by their father, who treated them as intellectual equals and encouraged them to read widely and freely. In their leisure time, Emily and her siblings created a number of fantasy worlds and began to write fiction. Emily's brother wrote *The Life of Alexander Percy*, which was to become the inspiration for *Wuthering Heights*. It tells how Alexander Percy and his wife had such a complete love and understanding of each other that eventually their love became self-destructive.

Star Crossed: Astrology, Personality Theory and the Meeting of Opposites

Emily remains a mysterious figure. She only left home occasionally, either to continue her education or to work as a schoolteacher, but she was always overcome by extreme homesickness, and would return home to Haworth as soon as she could.

Biographers have written that Emily was painfully shy, but had a clear head for logic, a stubborn tenacity and a strong will. One biographer's summary of her character is an excellent description of her natal chart. She had "a peculiar mixture of timidity and Spartan-like courage. Physically she was brave to a surprising degree. She loved few persons, but those few with a passion of self-sacrificing tenderness and devotion. To other people's failings she was understanding and forgiving, but over herself she kept a continual and most austere watch, never allowing herself to deviate for one instant from what she considered her duty."[ii]

In September 1848, when Emily was just thirty years old, her brother Branwell died suddenly. Less than three months later, Emily herself died, and it has been suggested that she died of a broken heart for the love of her brother.

Notes

1 There is evidence that some victims of abuse develop a special connection with their abusers. The term Stockholm Syndrome was coined in 1973 when four hostages were taken during a bank robbery in Stockholm, Sweden. During their captivity they developed a dependency on their captors and, after being released, they refused to testify in court against them. Similar attitudes have been found in victims of sexual abuse, human trafficking, terror and political and religious oppression.

2 The term Münchausen syndrome was first used in 1951 to describe a person who invents or exaggerates medical symptoms, sometimes engaging in self-harm, in order to gain attention or sympathy. The causes for developing this syndrome are believed to include early experiences of parents/caretakers who were emotionally unavailable for a variety of reasons. The very real experience of persistent but mysterious physical, mental or emotional symptoms, for

---

ii Eva Hope, (1886) *Queens of Literature of the Victorian Era*.

Virgo/Pisces: The Axis of Service

which no diagnosis can be found, can become a way of life, an unconscious attempt to gain the attention and care which was so lacking during childhood. 'Munchausen syndrome by proxy', on the other hand, describes a behaviour pattern in which a caregiver deliberately exaggerates, fabricates and/or induces physical, behavioural and/or mental health problems in those who are in their care. Typically perpetrated by a mother or female carer upon a child, this abuse is designed to elicit sympathy and attention for the so-called carer, who also derives the satisfaction of being able to deceive people whom they feel are more important or powerful than them. Perpetrators are known to switch medical providers frequently, until they find one that is willing to meet their level of need. Research has shown that many child victims continue the pattern of abuse with their own children. Using illness as a way of seeking attention and care can thus become a lifelong and multi-generational disorder.

3   The poet Elizabeth Barrett Browning had a Virgo Ascendant and five planets in Pisces in the sixth house (Mercury, Mars, Pluto, Sun and Venus). She was the first born of twelve children, all of whom were forbidden by their father to marry. He threatened to disown them if they disobeyed him. Elizabeth's early vitality and writing talent were clear to all, but her relationship to her father was one of vampire/victim: he was possessive, physically and psychically draining, and consumed her life force. Around the age of fifteen, Elizabeth developed an illness which the doctors were unable to diagnose. She had intense head and spinal pain, with a loss of mobility. The nature of her illness is still unclear.

Weak and frail, and living a reclusive life, Elizabeth nevertheless had a very strong will, and her illness excused her from the burdens of domestic duties expected of her sisters. She was free to devote herself entirely to a life of the mind, writing poetry from a young age, cultivating a wide correspondence and reading voraciously. As her literary reputation grew, she attracted the admiration of the writer Robert Browning, and so began one of the most famous courtships in literature. She and Robert fell deeply in love, a love which inspired some of the most enduring and beautiful poetry in the English language. This alliance enabled Elizabeth to escape from her psychically incestuous father. During their secret courtship, Elizabeth's health began to improve. She left her sick bed and learned to walk about her room, and then up and downstairs. They married secretly and a week later Elizabeth eloped with Robert, slipping out of the house with her maid, her dog and a small amount of luggage. They went to Paris and on to Italy, making their home in Florence, where they both continued to write. Elizabeth grew stronger and, at the age of 43, she gave birth to a son.

4   The singer Tina Turner has Neptune in Virgo in the second house, opposite Jupiter in Pisces in the eighth house, and Mars in Pisces in the seventh house.

Star Crossed: Astrology, Personality Theory and the Meeting of Opposites

The autobiographical film *What's Love Got To Do With It* tells the story of Tina's harrowing relationship with Ike, her manager and lover. Abandoned by her mother as a young child, Tina never felt safe or secure enough to decide for herself what was and what wasn't right for her. Developing a dependent, or co-dependent, adaptation, she was 'rescued' by Ike, her manager, and, at his insistence, promised never to leave him.

Ike managed the development of her successful career and Tina became a star, but he began to demand more and more from her, until she started taking drugs just to keep going. As her fame outgrew his, Ike became increasingly and brutally violent, repeatedly beating, choking and raping her as he continued to exploit her professionally. He spent all her money and humiliated her with his open infidelity. Tina was both a victim and a rescuer, and for some time she believed she could rescue the man who was beating and abusing her. She found it easier to feel his pain than to feel her own. Focusing on his vulnerability gave her some semblance of control. It took Tina twenty years to realise she didn't need Ike. As is often the case, the development of a transpersonal context or the discovery of spiritual beliefs can help people escape the interpersonal trap. Eventually, it was Tina's faith as a Buddhist which gave her the courage and strength to leave him. Selfless devotion to the other has to be a choice, not a trap. There are echoes of this same theme in the lives and relationships of singer/songwriters Whitney Houston and Carole King. See Carole King's autobiography *A Natural Woman* (Virago), published in April 2012.

Men are, of course, just as likely as women to enter into negative symbiotic relationships. The writer and playwright Oscar Wilde had Virgo/Pisces on the ASC/DES axis, with Neptune in Pisces conjunct his Descendant. He was consumed by, unable to escape from, and eventually destroyed by his tempestuous relationship with Lord Alfred Douglas, known as 'Bosie'. His relationship with 'Bosie' had all the hallmarks of a vampiric relationship from which he was never able to extract himself. It led to his trial and imprisonment for homosexuality, which was illegal at the time, and from which he never fully recovered. But Bosie was himself the victim of his vicious, sadistic, and quite possibly insane father, the Marquess of Queensberry. Neither were able to break this powerful pattern.

John Cleese, who wrote and starred in the TV series *Fawlty Towers*, loosely based on his own childhood experiences, has Virgo/Pisces on the ASC/DES axis and Neptune in Virgo in the first house. He played the character Basil Fawlty, a man who is consumed by impotent rage towards his wife, and yet completely unable to stand up to her. Hiding behind his submissive 'yes dear' persona, he resorts to a powerful display of passive aggression in a relationship which can only be described as vitriolic.

Virgo/Pisces: The Axis of Service

The Holiday is a 2006 romantic comedy with a happy ending. It tells the story of two characters, played by Kate Winslet and Jack Black, both caught in victim/rescuer relationships, and how, as the story develops, they find the confidence to stand up for themselves and break free from their old patterns.

5 In the 1999 film version of the book *The Talented Mr Ripley*, directed by Anthony Minghella, Matt Damon stars as Ripley, who gradually shapeshifts and assumes the character and identity of Dickie, played by Jude Law, his victim.

6 Bram Stoker's quintessential 1897 novel *Dracula* spawned an entire vampire genre, in books, films and television shows. The story of *The Phantom of the Opera* is a good example, first told in a novel by French writer Gaston Leroux, published in 1910. Andrew Lloyd Webber's 1986 musical adaptation of the book has been, and continues to be, a global phenomenon. The original London cast album has sold 40 million copies, becoming the biggest-selling cast album ever.

The story tells of Christine, a young soprano who fell under the spell of a disfigured and bitter musical genius who had hidden away for years in the sewers beneath the Paris Opera House in order to avoid the cruel stares of strangers. He was obsessed with Christine and became her tutor. Posing as the mysterious opera ghost, he terrorised the cast and crew until they agreed to give her the lead roles. With the Phantom's help, Christine became the venue's leading lady, but she had also become his creature.

When Christine fell in love with Raoul, a childhood sweetheart who was now the Opera's patron, the Phantom's despair quickly turned to rage. Driven insane with jealousy he kidnapped Christine and imprisoned her in his lair. When Raoul tracked down Christine he was himself overpowered and imprisoned by the Phantom. The Phantom gave Christine a difficult decision: if she chose to remain with him, Raoul would be allowed to go free, or if she chose her own freedom, then Raoul would die.

Under the spell of her jailer, Christine professed her love for him and decided to stay. By making this choice, she broke the unconscious collusion between them, which was too threatening for the Phantom to bear. Overcome by her decision, he freed both Christine and Raoul. Heartbroken, the Phantom escaped through a secret passage, leaving behind only his mask.

Lloyd Webber wrote the role of Christine specifically for Sarah Brightman, who became his second wife in 1984. He refused to allow his musical to open on Broadway unless she played the role. There are clear parallels in the relationship between the Phantom and Christine and the relationship between Andrew Lloyd Webber, the musical genius, and Sarah Brightman, his protégé, whom he raised to stardom.

Star Crossed: Astrology, Personality Theory and the Meeting of Opposites

Sarah Brightman's birth time is unknown, but her nodes span the Virgo/Pisces axis and she has a tight Venus Pluto conjunction in Virgo opposite Chiron in Pisces, which is conjunct Lloyd Webber's Mercury. He gave Sarah her voice and her international fame, but they had separated by 1990 when he left Sarah for another woman.

7 The poet and writer D H Lawrence wrote many stories on this theme, describing how, when love goes awry, the lovers become vampires to each other. If one is weak, the other will devour them. If both are strong, both may survive. He wrote:

> It is easy to see why each man kills the things he loves.
> To know a living thing is to kill it...
> To try to know a living being is to try to suck the life out of that being.
> The temptation of the vampire fiend, is this knowledge.
> The desirous consciousness, the spirit, is a vampire.

Lawrence had Mercury, Jupiter, Sun and North Node in Virgo, opposite the South Node in Pisces, and square Chiron and Pluto in Gemini in the eighth house. In addition, the intensity and possessiveness of his relationships is described by his Scorpio/Taurus ASC/DES, both square Mars in Cancer.

Chapter 9

Aries/Libra: Axis of Equilibrium

The Aries/Libra Axis

The Aries/Libra axis is ruled by Venus and Mars, mythic lovers and antagonists in equal measure. As the axis of equilibrium, it describes the inherent tension which exists in all relationships, the struggle to find a balance between autonomy and compromise, self-assertion and co-operation, passion and restraint. A healthy level of independence and self-determination are ultimately essential components in loving relationships. If this axis becomes particularly polarised then, as with all axes, one pole will gain the conscious upper hand, and the shadow or negative themes of the unconscious opposite pole will begin to dominate our behaviour.

The Mars ruled sign of Aries lacks awareness of others. Aries is spontaneous, instinctively competitive, driven by a compulsion to take action and not afraid to take risks. He is self-motivated and self-propelled, and automatically assumes the freedom to pursue his goals. People who identify exclusively with the Aries pole act quickly, without taking the time to consider the consequences of their actions. The story of Artemis, goddess of the hunt, and twin sister of Apollo, is a good example. Fiercely independent and competitive, Artemis' hunting companion, Orion, was her only love. One day, when Orion was swimming far off in a lake, Apollo challenged her skills as an archer, and rising immediately to the challenge, Artemis hit the target, unknowingly killing her lover.

The Venus ruled sign of Libra is driven by the need for balance and harmony in all things. Librans are natural arbitrators and mediators, and instinctively avoid confrontation or disputes. Taking their lead from others, they adapt by being accomplished and considerate, charming and accommodating. Their behaviour is usually defined by the social morality and ethics of the time, which tend to be irrelevant for Aries. At a young age, the Libran values of good behaviour and consideration for others are given the highest priority. The child receives positive reinforcement for being 'good', 'considerate', 'attractive' and 'accomplished', and negative reinforcement for being 'selfish' or 'self willed'.

An extreme Libran adaptation may have been caused originally by an early environment which was at war in some way, or in which the parents were in deep conflict. This can lead to a real fear of discord, anger or violence, which would have been experienced as threatening to their survival, and they may adapt by choosing to live solely for and through others, depending on them for direction, decision-making and focus. The price to be paid for identifying exclusively with the Libran end of the axis is a growing resentment and anger that they have sacrificed their own development and independence. It can take many years to recognise that they are, in fact, fiercely competitive, and to develop and integrate the courage and self-propelled independence of the Aries pole. Increasingly, they tend to find themselves surrounded by what they judge to be selfish, thoughtless people, who show no consideration for others. But the anger belongs to the thwarted and repressed Aries pole of this axis, and not to the sign of Libra itself.

If the Aries/Libra axis becomes radically split, so too does the ability to both love and desire the same person. The term 'object splitting' refers to people who frequently separate those whom they love romantically or protectively from those to whom they are sexually attracted. This sets the scene for competitive triangular relationships in adult life.

Systems theories generally accept Freud's work on psychosexual development, which tracks the changing focus of the libido during childhood and adolescence. Freud believed that, between the ages of three and five, the child becomes aware of himself 'in the system'. He begins to realise his separateness at a deep level and feels excluded from the parental relationship.

Children are naturally competitive and their initial experience of the 'primal triad' opens up the arena of object love and object rivalry, coined by Freud as the Oedipus complex. The child attempts to heal his exclusion from the parental relationship by competing with the parent of the same sex for the love of the parent of the opposite sex. A second Oedipal stage occurs at puberty, around the age of thirteen, with the period between being known as latency.

The innocent sensuality of the child needs to be accepted and gently managed at these delicate transitional times. The pleasure of physical contact, early sexual curiosity and arousal, enjoyment of attention and jealousy of the exclusive aspects of the parents' relationship are all normal developmental phases. The way the parents – and especially the parent of the opposite sex - handle the Oedipal stages is believed to be crucial for healthy psycho-sexual development.

Ideally, the parents will be capable of presenting a loving, united front to their child, demonstrating a clear differentiation between adult love and their love for their child. In such cases, the child will come to feel safe and secure within the family unit, and able to move through these stages reassured and valued in his own right, which prepares the ground for the development of loving and secure adult relationships.

In other words, it is important that the child experiences what is known as an Oedipal defeat. In an optimal environment he or she will fail to gain the allegiance of the parent of the opposite sex against the parent of the same sex. If the child is defeated in this attempt, but simultaneously accepted, appreciated and supported, then his emotional and psychosexual development can continue normally.

The Rejected or Exploited Child

In developmental theory, the Oedipal character style can become established if the child's natural sensuality and emerging sexuality is rejected, mishandled or exploited by one or both of the parents, normally the parent of the opposite sex. If the parent/s feel threatened and withdraw their affection, the child feels rejected, will come to believe there is something wrong with him, and feel sinful and guilty. But if the child's natural trust and affection are exploited, he will gradually build defensive structures designed to protect him from the **deep hurt** which accompanies this experience.

In extreme cases, one or both of the following character adaptations may emerge, although one pole is usually unconscious, and therefore autonomous.

Hysterical/Histrionic Adaptation

In seductive families, children are drawn into the conflict between their parents. Parents align themselves with the child of the opposite sex as a form of revenge, and/or as a subtle way of expressing anger against their partner. This is an Oedipal victory or triumph for the child, but the truth is that the child has been exploited, and used in the service of the adult carer's needs. An Oedipal triumph generates feelings of guilt in the child, the primary defence against which is dissociation, what Freud termed a 'splitting of consciousness' – with subsequent memory loss – a recognisable phenomenon in cases of child abuse, whether sexual or not.

Equally, if the parent of the same sex is absent, either physically or emotionally, the infant can become the symbolic partner of the parent of the opposite sex, such as 'mummy's little helper' or 'daddy's little princess', an Oedipal victory which is accompanied by premature feelings of omnipotence, in addition to suffering the guilt of the triumph. This is believed to set the pattern for repeated competitive relationships later in life.

With the repression of feelings of guilt into the unconscious, the person with a hysterical or histrionic adaptation 'acts out' in order to avoid any kind of 'feeling in'. Keeping relationships in a state of constant turmoil can be a self-protective act of displacement. Dramatic, artificial feelings are used as a shield against deeper, real feelings. They become attention-seeking, constantly demanding reassurance and approval, and over-sensitive to criticism. Unconscious hostility is expressed in repetitive 'game-like' interactions, and social skills are used to manipulate other people.

People with an hysterical/histrionic adaptation are generally lively, dramatic, enthusiastic and flirtatious, paying excessive attention to their physical appearance. Behavioural patterns include an addiction to drama, emotional immaturity and instability, an exaggeration of sexuality and inappropriate seductiveness, and intense rivalry and competition with members of the same sex. The underlying drive and motivation is often not so much about gaining the allegiance of the object of desire, but about the determination to win out against the presumed competitor.

Since competition and relationship triangles are so common on this axis, so too is sexual attraction to unavailable people for whom they compete, but lose interest in, should these same people become available. Equally, they may be very skilled in the initial seductive phases of a relationship but unable to sustain any interest as it becomes more intimate. Seeing themselves as sex objects, they treat their partners as sex objects. There is often no erotic involvement and sex takes place without intimacy, cut off from love and affection.

Rigid/Disciplined Adaptation

Alternatively, the rejected or exploited child may cut off from spontaneous desire and passion, and from sexual responsiveness which has become associated with rejection and guilt, and settle for acceptance and approval. People who sacrifice passion may be terrified of re-experiencing the emotional intensity, pain and guilt which was a feature of their seductive family background, and settle instead for relationships with tempered emotions. They learn to keep their passions and desires firmly under control, and strive to be conscientious, dutiful and morally correct. The development of exaggerated reserve and the observation of formal rules in relationships is a most culturally approved character style.

The internalised message, or defence structure, of the rigid/disciplined character style goes something like this: "I will win love and avoid future rejection by being good and dutiful" – a classic example of an extreme Libran adaptation. Tender feelings are blocked or expressed indirectly, if at all.

In the primal triad, the excluded party - most commonly the mother in seductive father/daughter relationships - often adopts a rigid/disciplined role 'in the system' and becomes cold, distant or hostile. Many women in seductive family systems feel that their mothers have to some degree sacrificed them to their fathers, while at the same time being grimly determined to preserve their marriage at all costs.

There is a fear of doing the wrong thing, and the resulting development of an inhibited **false self**, doing everything by the book, obeying social conventions and adopting socially approved attitudes and behaviours. Value systems are adopted, formal and rigid, as they impose strict rules and expectations on themselves and others. The spontaneous life force of Aries or Mars is firmly denied, suppressed, controlled or projected, kept at arm's length by a stance of righteousness. Anger, hatred and competition are denied, and anything passionate, sensual or self-indulgent is kept under tight control and harshly judged when observed in others. Relationships can also be formed with people who do the 'acting out' for them, which allows them to retain the moral high ground.

They can even incite or provoke others to act out, usually unconsciously, while denying any involvement. The extreme Libran characteristics of chronic indecision, vacillation, obsessive doubt and procrastination can plague even the simplest activities, related to the fear of doing the wrong thing. There can be much 'displacement activity' – a shifting of attention to peripheral details – as well as the use of rationalisation and/or abstract justifications. Much attention is given to the proper role behaviour, but these relationships are often characterised by hidden, unconscious competition and power struggles.

This splitting of consciousness can lead to the construction of dissociated or at least unintegrated double lives, one 'good' and one 'bad'. The 'good' boy or girl is charming and well behaved, with a strong moral compass. But somewhere the 'bad' boy or girl will have to find expression. The underlying rage of the thwarted and blocked Aries shadow will inevitably find a way to express itself. A not unusual outlet for the hostility of the now distorted Mars energy can be the sadistic, dominant and strict exercise of authority.[1]

The excluded, rejected and now unconscious Mars energy can become autonomous. The person may, for example, lead a secret sex life or be addicted to pornography or other forms of voyeurism. Intrusive thoughts, especially of a hostile or sexually sadistic nature, can become problematic, and troublesome obsessive thoughts and compulsive behaviours seem to take on a life of their own. A blocked Mars turns inwards, against itself, and it is not unusual for people with an extremely moral, intellectual or rigid adaptation to have recurring nightmares of murderers, or be tormented by images of rape and carnage. Addictions such as compulsive spending, eating disorders and dissociated promiscuity can also be outlets for the blocked Mars energy.

Star Crossed: Astrology, Personality Theory and the Meeting of Opposites

An example from my own practice concerns a client with Sun, Mercury and Venus in Libra, but also Mars in Aquarius on the MC opposite Pluto in Leo on the IC. She was an experienced and dedicated therapist, devoted to her clients and working to improve the provision of social services for families in need, as well as being active in several psychotherapeutic groups. In other words, she was strongly identified with her Libran Sun and Mars in Aquarius on the MC. But she was becoming more aware of some really deep anger and buried rage. With Pluto on the IC we would expect this to be an inherited, although unacknowledged, aspect of the family system. My client was not an astrologer and, much to her surprise, and with some embarrassment, she had become attracted, even addicted, to watching the Terminator films, in which Arnold Schwarzenegger can be seen as a personification of Pluto. Watching these films again and again, she was getting in touch with the brute force and power of Pluto within her own nature and, by encountering this archetype through story, she was in fact doing her own therapy. These films provided her with the opportunity to engage with, work through and eventually integrate the Mars/Pluto opposition in her chart, and would continue to be important to her until the emotions associated with this configuration had been released and finally 'used up'.

One way of preserving a stable love relationship which lacks passion is to deflect the erotic involvement onto a variety of socially acceptable alternatives, such as one's career, or onto a hobby or other passion, such as gardening, pets, motor bikes, flamenco dancing, or any number of alternative relationships which are 'safe', and which can often lead to exceptional achievements and creative expression, but which nevertheless have an element of obsession and compulsion attached to them. In this way, the drive of the Aries pole finds a creative, passionate but unthreatening outlet.

Escaping into romantic fantasy is another relatively safe way of experiencing powerful passions and emotions removed from every-day life.

An erotic involvement with fictional characters can become compulsive and addictive, even psychically promiscuous, without threatening the status quo. The Oedipal triangle is preserved without rocking the boat.

Aries – Libra Stories

Stories on the Aries/Libra axis usually include themes of intense rivalry and competition in love, and the consequences of the choices we make. The attainment, or painful renunciation, of love has always provided powerful inspiration for enduring works of art or music. Stories, books and films in this genre are ways of entering, in projection, an erotic and passionate fantasy world. But they may well serve an important therapeutic function, a way of processing the decisions we make in our own lives.[2]

With the emphasis on the Libran pole of this axis, there is usually a stable and dutiful partnership, which lacks passion, and a carefully concealed adulterous affair or substitute relationship which breaks the social code. In an attempt to preserve the status quo, the cover up normally involves a web of lies. Common themes include rationalisation, justification and sacrifice to a higher moral or spiritual purpose, or to avoid hurting others. Guilt overwhelms desire and a sense of morality preserves feelings of righteousness. The renunciation of passion raises the romantic and erotic fantasy to a higher moral or spiritual level and, in the process, removes any guilt. There are many famous and enduring films in this genre.[3]

In stories with an emphasis on the Aries pole of this axis, the hero or heroine breaks the rules and follows their desires, as a consequence of which they usually find themselves ostracised and rejected by their community. There are many stories about the people, almost always women, who sacrifice social respectability to pursue an impossible, tragic love, stories which often end with hardship and ruin, separation, mourning and loss.[4]

Star Crossed: Astrology, Personality Theory and the Meeting of Opposites

Tristan and Isolde

The legend of **Tristan and Isolde** tells the tragic story of the adulterous love between the Cornish knight Tristan and the Irish princess Isolde. Since its first appearance in the twelfth century, it has been retold again and again, and has been the subject of many works of art, operas, plays and films.

Figure 14 Tristan and Isolde.

The story takes place during the reign of King Arthur. Isolde, daughter of the King of Ireland, was betrothed to King Mark of Cornwall. King Mark sent his nephew, Tristan, to Ireland to escort Isolde back to Cornwall, but on their voyage back they – knowingly or unknowingly - drank a magic potion with aphrodisiac properties. This had been given to Isolde by her mother, and intended for Isolde and King Mark to drink on their wedding night. Tristan and Isolde fell in love and, even after her marriage to King Mark, the couple continued their clandestine love affair. When Mark discovered it, he forgave Isolde but Tristan was banished from Cornwall.

In France, Tristan met the Duke of Brittany's daughter, Iseult, and was attracted to her because of the similarity of her name to his true love. He married her, but did not consummate the marriage, because of his love for the 'true' Isolde. Falling seriously ill, he sent for Isolde in the hope that their reunion would cure him. If she agreed to come, the returning ship's sails would be white, but if she did not agree the sails would be black. Iseult, seeing the white sails, lied to Tristan and told him that the sails were black. This is a perfect example of the underlying power of the Oedipal triangle which threatens so many relationships. The competition between two men or two women for the object of their mutual desire is an archetypal theme, and one which is usually central to these stories. When Iseult conveyed to Tristan the false message that the sails were black, he died of grief before Isolde could reach him, and Isolde died soon after of a broken heart.

William Morris

Remarkable parallels can be drawn between this story and the well-known triangular relationship between the artists William Morris, Dante Gabriel Rossetti, and their model, Jane Burden, with whom both men fell in love. The Oxford Union murals which they painted in the mid-nineteenth century depict scenes from Arthurian myth, including the story of Tristan and Isolde, and Sir Lancelot's Vision of the Holy Grail. Lancelot is, perhaps, best known for his adulterous relationship with Guinevere, King Arthur's queen.

Figure 15 William Morris

William Morris was a textile and book designer, poet, novelist, publisher and a leading force in the foundation of the British Arts and Crafts movement, which was devoted to the preservation of traditional craft skills. He developed a keen interest in the romanticism and chivalric values of the Arthurian middle ages, which he deemed greatly preferable to the industrial capitalism of Britain's Victorian era. He wrote and translated

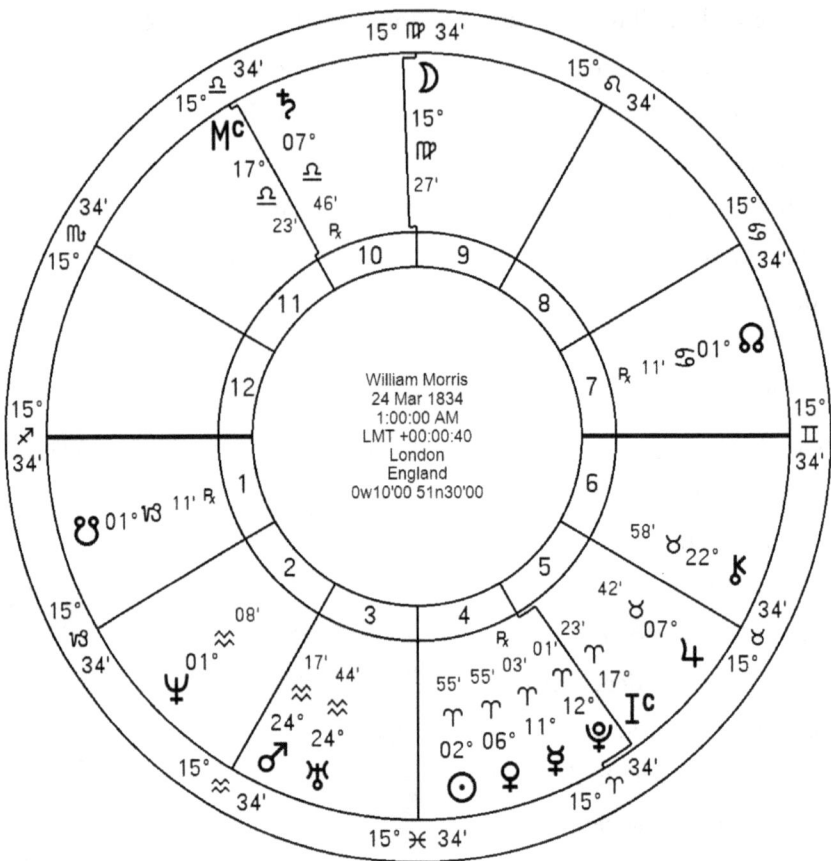

many epic poems, novels and fantasy romances, and his designs, like the work of the Pre-Raphaelite painters with whom he was associated, frequently included medieval motifs.

It was at Oxford that Morris met Edward Burne-Jones who became his lifelong friend and collaborator. Burne-Jones was one of the founders of the Pre-Raphaelite brotherhood, along with Dante Gabriel Rossetti. After university, Morris founded a decorative arts firm with Burne-Jones, Rossetti and others, which became highly fashionable and much in demand, with Morris designing tapestries, wallpaper, fabrics, furniture, and stained glass windows.

Aries/Libra: Axis of Equilibrium

The Aries/Libra axis often signifies remarkable artistic talent and ability, and William Morris was no exception. He was one of the most significant cultural figures in Victorian Britain and the force of his genius has never been questioned. The Aries/Libra axis is strongly emphasised in his chart and its many themes are clearly reflected in his life.[i] Biographers have described Morris as industrious, honest, fair-minded, unaffected and business-like, with a loud voice and a nervous restless manner. He spoke to the point and with remarkable clear good sense, and was widely admired for his integrity. But his behaviour could also be erratic. He had a wild temper and, when sufficiently enraged, would suffer seizures and blackouts.[ii] But Morris also exhibited a strong sense of responsibility towards his family, and did not allow people to 'penetrate the central part of him'.[iii]

In 1857, while engaged in the painting of the Oxford Union murals, Morris and Rossetti attended a theatre performance at which a young woman called Jane Burden was also present. Rossetti was struck by Jane's appearance, and decided that she would make a perfect Queen Guinevere. Jane agreed to sit for him as his model, and Morris later painted a portrait of her as the tragic Arthurian princess Isolde, in *La Belle Iseult*, now in the Tate Gallery.

During this time, both Rossetti and Morris fell in love with Jane, but Rossetti was already engaged to Lizzie Siddal, another of the group's models who appears in many Pre-Raphaelite paintings, including John Everett Millais's famous *Ophelia*.

William and Jane were married in 1859, and Rossetti and Lizzie were married the following year, in 1860. But, as Rossetti confided to a friend shortly before his death, his marriage was a commitment undertaken "out

---

i   MC/IC axis in Libra/Aries, with Sun, Venus, Mercury, Pluto stellium in Aries in the fourth house, all opposing Saturn in Libra in the tenth house.
ii Mars, the ruler of the Aries stellium, is exactly conjunct Uranus in Aquarius in the third house.
iii Saturn in Libra in the tenth house.

of a mistaken sense of loyalty and fear of giving pain", when in truth his heart had been lost to another.[5]

After his wife's death in 1862, Jane became Rossetti's favourite model and muse, inspiring some of his best poetry and paintings. Whatever the extent of their relationship, they were clearly on emotionally intimate terms for many years, while Morris increasingly focused on the running of his thriving interior-design company.

Jane's liaison with Rossetti is infamous. By the late 1860s gossip had spread around London, where they were regularly seen spending time together. In June 1871, Morris and Rossetti entered into a joint tenancy of Kelmscott Manor in the Cotswolds. This may have been an indication of Morris' desire to remove themselves from public scrutiny and keep things civilised for all concerned. If he suffered from jealousy or insecurity, he kept it to himself. His graciousness was not lost on Jane, who once praised him as "the most magnanimous, the least selfish of men."

Figure 16 Jane Burden as Persephone, Dante Gabriel Rossetti 1874

Morris divided his time between London and Kelmscott, but never spent more than a few days at a time at Kelmscott when Rossetti was there. In the summer of 1871 Morris visited Iceland for two months, leaving Jane, his two daughters and Rossetti at Kelmscott. During this period, Rossetti painted at least eight versions of Jane as the mythic Prosperine, or Persephone, a woman who had been abducted against her will into marriage with the lord of the underworld, Hades/Pluto, a theme laden with symbolism for Rossetti.

Aries/Libra: Axis of Equilibrium

By 1874 Morris' friendship with Rossetti had seriously eroded, and their acrimonious falling out led Rossetti to leave Kelmscott. Jane's relationship with Rossetti continued through correspondence and occasional visits, but his dependence on drugs and alcohol and increasing paranoia eventually led her to distance herself from him. Rossetti died in 1882 at the age of fifty three. In 1883 Jane was introduced to the poet Wilfrid Blunt, with whom she embarked on a second affair, which Morris may have been aware of.

Notes

1 Nurse Ratchet in the film *One Flew Over The Cuckoo's Nest* and Dolores Umbridge in the Harry Potter film *Order of the Phoenix*, are good examples of women whose official positions provide them with the opportunity to be cruel and sadistic. The novelist Stephen King wrote in a 2003 review that Dolores Umbridge was the "greatest make-believe villain to come along since Hannibal Lecter". The actress Imelda Staunton, who played the role of Umbridge, commented that both she, and every fan of the series, hated her character.

2 A real-life example is that of the musician and blues guitarist Eric Clapton. Clapton's Sun is in Aries in the sixth house and his Mercury in Aries is on his DES. With Libra/Aries on his ASC/DES axis, he has an exact Moon Venus opposition across his first and seventh houses, both square Pluto in Leo on the MC. His close friendship with the Beatle George Harrison brought him into contact with Harrison's wife, Pattie Boyd, with whom he became deeply infatuated. His unrequited love and desire inspired some of his most brilliant, moving and enduring work, and provided most of the material for the album *Layla and Other Assorted Love Songs* (1970). Clapton drew the story of Layla from a classical Persian poem which tells of a young man who fell hopelessly in love with a beautiful, unavailable woman and who went crazy because he could not marry her. Clapton's passionate feelings for Pattie Boyd are immortalised in his song *Wonderful Tonight*.

Clapton started living with Pattie Boyd in 1974, and George Harrison's *Dark Horse* album of the same year contains his own songs about this painful period, such as *So Sad* and *Simply Shady*. Clapton and Pattie Boyd married in 1979 but, as is often the case with triangular relationship patterns, he began another relationship with Yvonne Kelly five years later, although both were married to other partners at the time.

Star Crossed: Astrology, Personality Theory and the Meeting of Opposites

3 In the enduringly popular film *Brief Encounter*, a seemingly happy wife and mother accidentally meets a stranger while waiting for a train. They are passionately drawn to each other, but in the end she realises she can't leave her family – the guilt would be unbearable.

Graham Greene's novel *The End of the Affair* has been made into a film starring Julianne Moore (Sarah), her husband Stephen Rea (Henry) and the man she passionately loves, played by Ralph Fiennes (Maurice). The story hinges on a wartime event when a bomb explodes in the building in which Sarah and Maurice are conducting their adulterous affair, and Sarah believes that Maurice has been killed. She makes a desperate pact with God, promising to renounce her affair if Maurice is restored to life. To her amazement she then discovers that Maurice has not died, but she keeps her bargain with God and chooses to live without the passion which has given meaning to her life.

In the film *The Bridges of Madison County*, Francesca (played by Meryl Streep) leaves a letter to her children at her death asking for her ashes to be tossed from a nearby covered bridge. She writes about the four most important days of her life and the love she sacrificed for them. A handsome stranger (Clint Eastwood) passed through her neighbourhood and reawakened her dormant passion and desire. They became lovers, but Francesca decided that she could not leave with him or live with the guilt. It would destroy her husband's love and undermine everything she has taught her children about family and fidelity.

A more chilling example of complete dissociation on this axis is that of *The Stepford Wives,* in which the Stepford Men's Club replace their real wives with robots who, on the one hand, are perfect home makers, totally compliant and obedient, and on the other hand, sexual objects and playthings who fulfil all their sexual fantasies and desires.

4 *Madame Bovary*, *Lady Chatterley's Lover* and *Anna Karenina* are good examples. Tolstoy's great nineteenth-century novel, *Anna Karenina*, tells the story of a woman in a respectable, socially sanctioned marriage. She met and embarked upon an affair with the handsome officer Count Vronsky and did the unthinkable in Russian society, abandoning the security and status of her marriage to be with him. Socially ostracised, Anna was no longer allowed to see her son, which caused her great suffering. As Vronsky began to distance himself from her passionate attachment, Anna gradually became more jealous and hysterical. She had lost everything and ended her life by throwing herself under a train.

5 Jane was born on 19th October 1839 in Oxford, England. Her birth time is unknown, but her triangular relationships are clear from her strong Aries/Libra emphasis. Jane has Venus in Libra and a tight Sun, Mercury, Jupiter stellium, also in Libra, opposite Pluto in Aries.

Aries/Libra: Axis of Equilibrium

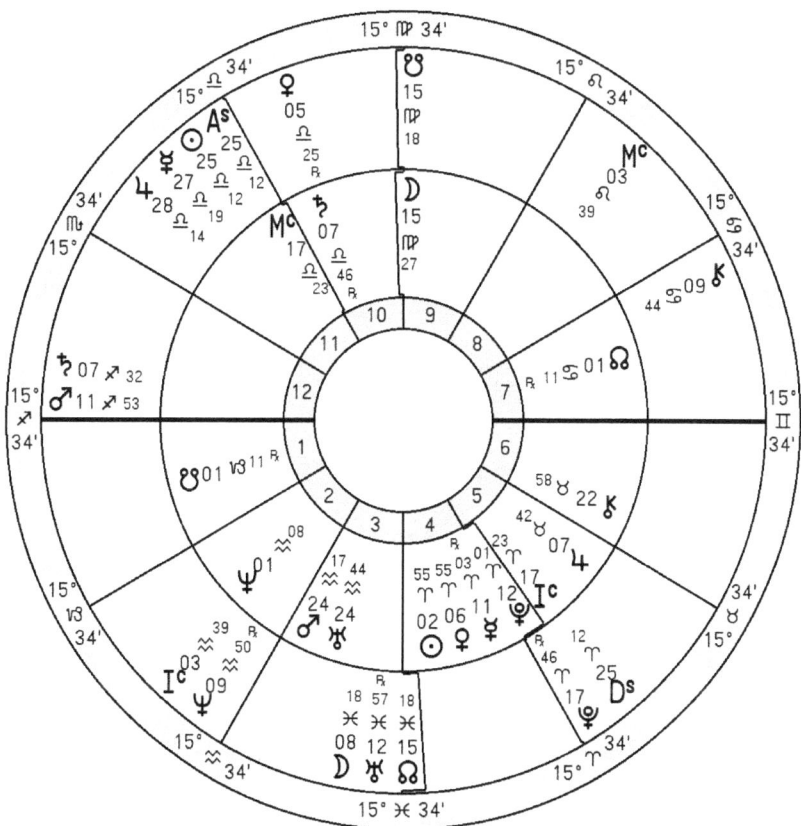

William Morris (inner chart)/Jane Burden (outer chart) biwheel

There is a powerful synastry between Jane and William's birth charts. Jane's Venus is conjunct William's Saturn in Libra and opposite his Sun Venus Mercury Pluto stellium in Aries. Her Pluto is exactly on his IC, suggesting the intensity of Jane's power over William. His Moon is exactly on Jane's South Node in Virgo, describing his idealisation of the perfect woman, but Jane has a Moon Uranus conjunction on her North Node in Pisces signifying, perhaps, her need to escape from the confines of William's overwhelming projections onto her as his muse.

Star Crossed: Astrology, Personality Theory and the Meeting of Opposites

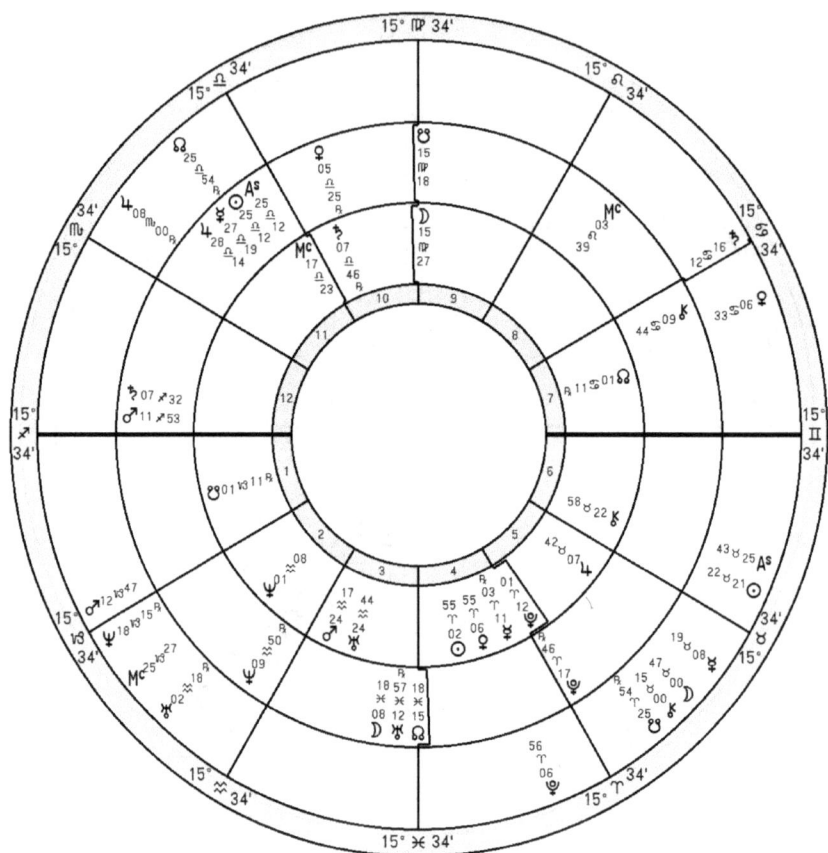

William Morris (inner chart)/Jane Burden (middle chart)/
Gabriel Dante Rossetti (outer chart)

As we would expect, the synastry between Jane and Rossetti is also significant. Rossetti's North Node, which so often describes a sense of personal fate and destiny, is exactly conjunct Jane's Sun Mercury Jupiter stellium in Libra. Rossetti's Pluto in Aries is opposite Jane's Venus and William's Saturn in Libra, signifying the hidden and taboo nature of their relationship, and describing William's role in the triad, as he continued to do his duty and support his wife and marriage, and ignored, or failed to challenge, the relationship going on under his roof. Jane's uncomfortable and painful position as a woman caught between her values of marriage and family and her personal passions is described by her Chiron in Cancer, conjunct Rossetti's Venus. Conversely, Jane's Venus and Rossetti's Sun ASC conjunction fall on William's sensitive Chiron in Taurus, which describes his wish to preserve stability and possibly his sadness and pain in the face of his wife's infidelity.

However, picking up the Oedipal theme of the Aries/Libra axis, it may be that competition between the two men lay at the root of this triangular relationship. Rossetti's Pluto is conjunct William's Aries stellium, and opposes his Saturn. Additionally, Rossetti's Saturn in Cancer tightly squares William's Aries/Libra MC/IC axis, ultimately challenging, threatening and restricting both William's business enterprises and the stability of his family. There are other contacts between the two men: such as Rossetti's Uranus conjunct William's Neptune, their opposed Jupiters, and William's Chiron on Rossetti's Sun ASC conjunction in Taurus (echoes of the intensely possessive Taurus/Scorpio axis?)

Epilogue

Love Actually

The film *Love Actually* was written and directed by Richard Curtis, and released in November 2003 to generally mixed reviews. But it has gradually become a perennial seasonal favourite, and remains one of the most popular romantic comedies of the last twenty years, testament to its archetypal resonance.

The film follows the lives of nine very different couples in a series of loosely interrelated tales, taking place during the month before Christmas. Each story is a fine example of the character styles identified by personality theory and encountered in the relationship themes of the six astrological axes. Some of the stories describe rites of passage which lead to the resolution of inherent conflicts, some have happy endings and some leave the outcome painfully unresolved. The film reflects the relationship patterns discussed in the previous chapters which, to a greater or lesser extent, we recognise in ourselves and in others.

Two of the stories pick up themes commonly found on the **Cancer/ Capricorn** axis; stories of loneliness and belonging, and the painful experience of working through bereavement and grief, following the loss of a loved one.

The story of aging rock-and-roll legend Billy Mack (Bill Nighy) and his longtime friend and manager Joe (Gregor Fisher) tracks the events leading up to the release of a variation of the old pop song 'Love is All Around'. Joe hopes that it will become the Christmas number one single and, in a bid for sales of what is generally acknowledged to be a questionable re-release, Billy promises to perform it in the nude if he is successful. This catches the public imagination and the song does indeed reach the number one position. Invited to a party hosted by Sir Elton John, Billy feels alone and out of place. He leaves the party and chooses to spend the evening instead with Joe, his oldest and dearest friend, with whom he feels safe and comfortable and who is, in fact, the only family he has.

The story of Daniel (Liam Neeson) and Sam (Thomas Sangster) is one of shared bereavement and grief, and the gradual transition to new love. At the start of the film, Daniel and his stepson Sam are both mourning, in their own ways, the death of Joanna, Daniel's wife and Sam's mother. Sam has fallen in love with an American schoolmate called Joanna (Olivia Olson), who has the same name as his mother. He wishes above all to gain her attention and, with this in mind, and with Daniel's support, he learns how to play the drums and joins the school orchestra for the big Christmas pageant finale, in which Joanna is the lead singer. Afterwards, he is downhearted, believing that he has missed his chance to make an impression on Joanna and, as she leaves with her mother to catch a plane back to America, Daniel convinces Sam to show her how he feels. They race to the airport and Sam runs through the security checks and catches up with Joanna, who acknowledges him by name and kisses him on the cheek. This farewell gives Sam a happy ending which will help him move on after his mother's death. Meanwhile, Daniel meets Carol (Claudia Schiffer), the mother of one of Sam's schoolmates, and it seems that he, too, may well find new love.

At the end of the film, Sam greets Joanna at Heathrow Airport, as she returns from America with her mother. He is accompanied by Daniel, his new girlfriend Carol, and her son, evidence that Daniel, too, has moved on and that they have created a new family.

The story of John and Judy is an interesting take on the **Taurus/Scorpio** axis. John (Martin Freeman) and Judy (Joanna Page) are professional film stand-ins. They meet on set, where they are required to simulate sex scenes for the camera crew. Initially, their relationship belongs to the Taurus end of this axis, since they are doing the job simply for the money; it is all part of a normal day's work. This is a classic example of the sex-for-money theme so prevalent on this axis. In this example, the Scorpio end of the axis is entirely projected onto the subject matter of the film they are involved with. Positive clues are there from the beginning, since, in integrated Taurus/Scorpio relationships, there is an equal balance of power and an equal exchange of personal resources, both financial and emotional. This depends on each party having sufficient levels of self-respect and self-esteem. In spite of their personal shyness off-set, John and Judy begin to feel genuine affection for one another, and this axis begins to find its balance, leading to the integration of both poles of this axis. At the end of the film we see the couple, now newlyweds, heading off to their honeymoon.

There are two stories illustrating the relationship patterns found on the **Gemini/Sagittarius** axis, both of which tell of the attraction between people from different cultures and languages. The first concerns Jamie (Colin Firth) and Aurélia (Lúcia Moniz). Betrayed by his girlfriend, Jamie retreats to a cottage in France to write a novel, a suitably Gemini theme, where he is introduced to Aurélia, his Portuguese housekeeper, who does not speak English. Right from the start, the Gemini/Sagittarius themes are evident; there is a significant age difference, and they have different cultures, languages and comparative social standing. Despite their inability to communicate, they become attracted to each other. When Jamie returns to England, he decides to learn Portuguese, and at the same time Aurelia decides to learn English. Realizing he has no wish to join his family at Christmas – the very prospect makes him feel trapped – he returns to France, tracks Aurelia down in the restaurant where she is working, and in broken Portuguese, declares his love for her and proposes. She accepts, in broken English and the crowd erupts in applause.

The second story with clear Gemini/Sagittarius themes also illustrates the attraction between people from different cultures and languages, in this case between the English spoken on different sides of the Atlantic.

After unsuccessfully attempting to woo various English women, Colin Frissell (Kris Marshall) decides he is on the wrong continent and informs his friend Tony (Abdul Salis) that he plans to go to America, convinced that his Britishness will be an asset. Landing in Milwaukee, Wisconsin, Colin visits a bar, where he meets three attractive girls who fall for his English accent. At the end of the film, they all return to London and, at Heathrow Airport, Colin introduces them to his astonished friend.

The story of David and Natalie is a classic example of the polarities encountered on the **Leo/Aquarius** relationship axis. David (Hugh Grant), who initially represents the Aquarius pole, is the recently elected British Prime Minister. Still unmarried, it is clear that his political career has taken priority in his life, and that his success and high profile in public service have been achieved at the cost of his personal life. As his sister, Karen, tells him, he is now far too important to have time for his family.

Natalie (Martine McCutcheon) is a new junior member of the household staff at 10 Downing Street, representing the Leo pole. She has none of the sophistication of his own background, but is spontaneous, open and heart-centered, and prone to a range of social faux pas. David and Natalie are immediately attracted to one another.

During a meeting with the U.S. President (Billy Bob Thornton), David is enraged to catch him making inappropriate advances to Natalie. At the following joint press conference, David is uncharacteristically assertive and takes a stand against the President's intimidating policies. At this point the roles change; David's speech is pure Leo, as he defends the UK against the power and arrogance of the US President (now in the Aquarius role), pointing out that true friendship does not involve bullying. David's speech receives a great reception from his office and from the press, when he reminds everyone of the pride and achievements of Great Britain.

Disturbed by his attraction to Natalie, David arranges to have her reassigned to another position in which their paths will no longer cross but, as Christmas approaches, Natalie sends David a Christmas card declaring that she is his and no one else's. Spurred to action, David tracks Natalie down, and their first kiss is witnessed by the entire audience at the school pageant when the stage curtains are drawn back. At the end of the film Natalie welcomes David when he arrives at Heathrow Airport, in full view of the press, indicating that their relationship is now publicly revealed.

A classic **Virgo/Pisces** story is told in the symbiotic relationship between Sarah and her brother Michael. Sarah (Laura Linney) works at Harry's graphic design company (a suitably Virgo/Pisces setting) and has been in love for years with the company's creative director, Karl (Rodrigo Santoro). They finally connect at the firm's Christmas party and he drives her home, but as usual, Michael, Sarah's mentally ill brother, keeps phoning her, and the evening tryst is aborted. This is a particularly sad and painful story – Sarah has identified, most likely from a young age, with the role of rescuer and carer. She and Michael are in a mutually dependent relationship, which excludes the possibility of any other relationships for Sarah. She feels she has no choice but to put Michael first and to sacrifice her chance of personal happiness. At the end of the film Sarah pays a Christmas visit to Michael, in the psychiatric hospital where he lives. Michael attacks her and has to be restrained.

There are two stories about marriages and about the triangular relationships so commonly found on the **Aries/Libra** axis. The first tells of Mark (Andrew Lincoln), Peter (Chiwetel Ejiofor) and Juliet (Keira Knightley), whom both men love. Mark plays the Libra role. He is Peter's best friend, and best man at Peter's wedding. But he is in love with Juliet (Keira Knightley), the bride. In order to protect himself, he adopts a defensive stance, feigning coldness to distance himself from Juliet, evading her requests to see the video he made at the wedding. But when she finds and watches the video, which is almost entirely of her, she realizes that Mark is in love with her. He is caught on the double bind between his loyalty to his friend, Peter, and his love for Juliet. As the excluded party in this triangle, he chooses not to reveal his feelings, or to rock the boat.

Closure for Mark comes at the end of the film when, under cover as a carol-singer, he shows Juliet a series of cue cards, on which he has written, without expectation of reciprocation, that he loves her. As he walks away, Juliet runs after him and gives him a quick kiss before returning inside.

In the story of Harry, Karen and Mia, the triangular relationship themes so common on the Aries/Libra axis are defined by the two women. Harry (Alan Rickman) is the managing director of a design agency. He is married to Karen (Emma Thompson), who has chosen to live a classic Libran supporting role to her husband, and to be a full-time mother to their two children. There are clues that she has sacrificed her own potential and career development in order to do so.

Mia is Harry's new secretary/PA, and it is clear from the beginning that she is set on competing for, and seducing, the previously faithful Harry. Mia's character makes an interesting case study, since she embarks upon recreating what is likely to have been her own childhood experience of being caught in a seductive Oedipal triangle, as 'daddy's little princess'. She shows all the signs of a rejected or exploited child, addicted to drama and 'acting out' in order to avoid any kind of 'feeling in', most likely as a self-protective act of displacement. Mia is a 'game player', intensely competitive with other women. She is attention-seeking, manipulative and inappropriately seductive. Seeing herself as a sex object, she treats others as sex objects. It seems likely that Mia's pattern is to engage in repeated competitive relationships and that, should she gain Harry's allegiance, and win the competition with Karen, she will lose interest in him and move on to her next conquest.

At the company's Christmas party, at which Mia is dressed as a devil, she dances closely with Harry, in the presence of his wife. Karen immediately recognizes Mia's intentions and warns Harry about them.

As Christmas approaches, Karen discovers an expensive necklace in Harry's coat pocket and happily assumes it is a gift for her. But when the family open their presents, she is heartbroken when she receives a different present, and realizes that the necklace was bought for someone else. She confronts Harry and tells him he has made a mockery of their marriage and of her. At this point in the story, Karen has a choice. If she can weather the storm, and continue to put Harry and her family first, she can at least retain the moral high ground, which is some sort of compensation for those to adopt a Libran role, but at the cost of owning the Aries pole of this axis, which would involve taking action, regaining her independence and, perhaps, finding renewed passion in her life. In the film, Karen continues to put on a happy face and acts as if nothing is wrong in front of her children, her peers, and everyone at the Christmas pageant. At the end of the film, the viewer is left to wonder what is next for the couple.

Chart Data

Assange, Julian	3 July 1971, 3.00pm AEST, Townsville, Australia
Barrett Browning, Elizabeth	6 March 1806, 7.00pm LMT, Kellow, near Durham, England.
Barrie, J.M.	9 May 1860, 6.42am GMT, Kirriemuir, Angus, Scotland
Boyd, Patti	17 March 1944, 4.00am GDT, Taunton, England
Brightman, Sarah	14 August 1960, time unknown, London, England
Brontë, Emily	30 July 1818, 2.49pm LMT, Thornton, England
Burden, Jane	19 October 1839, time unknown, Oxford, England
Campbell, Joseph	26 March 1904, 7.25pm EST, White Plains, NY, USA
Clapton, Eric	30 March 1945, 8.45pm GDT, Ripley, Surrey, England
Claudel, Camille	8 December 1864, 5.00am LMT, Fere en Tardenois, France
Cleese, John	27 October 1939, 3.15am BST, Weston-super-Mare, England
Close, Glenn	19 March 1947, 2.12pm EST, Greenwich, CT, USA

Costner, Kevin	18 January 1955, 9.40pm PST, Lynwood, CA, USA
Cruise, Tom	3 July 1962, time unknown, Syracuse, NY, USA
Cumberbach, Benedict	19 July 1976, 12.00pm GDT, Hammersmith, England
Dickens, Charles	7 February 1812, 7.50pm LMT, Portsmouth, England
Douglas, Michael	25 September 1944, 10.30am EWT, New Brunswick, NJ, USA
Fritzl, Josef	9 April 1935, 3.04pm CET-1, Amstetten, Austria
Garbo, Greta	18 September 1905, 7.30pm MET, Stockholm, Sweden
Hoffman, Dustin	8 August 1937, 5.07pm PST, Los Angeles, USA
Hopkins, Anthony	31 December 1937, 9.15am GMT, Port Talbot, Wales
Irons, Jeremy	19 September 1948, 2.00am GDT, Ventnor, England
Jung, Carl	26 July 1875, 7.24pm BMT, Kesswil, Switzerland
Jung, Emma	30 March 1882, 10.45pm LMT, Schaffhausen, Switzerland
Kipling, Rudhyard	30 December 1865, 10.00pm LMT, Bombay, India
Lawrence, Jennifer	15 August 1990, 3.20pm EDT, Louisville, KY, USA
Maar, Dora	22 November 1907, 2.30am PMT, Paris, France

Morris, William	24 March 1834, 1.00am LMT, London, England
Nilsen, Dennis	23 November 1945, 5.05pm GMT, Fraserburgh, Scotland
Picasso, Pablo	25 October 1881, 11.15pm LMT, Malaga, Spain
Proust, Marcel	10 July 1871, 11.30pm LMT, Paris, France
Rodin, Auguste	12 Nov 1840, 12 noon LMT, Paris, France
Rossetti, Dante Gabriel	12 May 1828, 4.30am LMT, London, England
Turner, Tina	26 November 1939, 10.10pm CST, Nutbush, TN, USA
Turing, Alan	23 June 1912, 2.15am GMT, London, England
West, Frederick	29 September 1941, 8.30am BST, Ledbury, England
Wilde, Oscar	16 October 1854, 3.00am LMT, Dublin, Ireland

Bibliography

Assagioli, Roberto (1965) *Psychosynthesis,* New York: The Viking Press

(1967) *Jung and Psychosynthesis,* New York: Psychosynthesis Research Foundation

(1973) *The Act of Will,* New York: Penguin Books.

Bertine, Eleanor (1992) *Close Relationships: Family, Friendship, Marriage,* Inner City Books

Bolen, Jean Shinoda (2014) *Goddesses in Everywoman: Powerful Archetypes in Women's Lives,* Harper PB Thirtieth Anniversary Edition

(2014) *Gods in Everyman: Archetypes that Shape Men's Lives,* Harper PB Thirtieth Anniversary Edition

Campbell, Joseph (2017) *The Hero with a Thousand Faces,* Joseph Campbell Foundation

Cater, Nancy (2005) *Cinema and Psyche,* Spring Journal: A Journal of Archetype and Culture

Clay, Catrine (2015) *Labyrinths: Emma Jung, Her Marriage to Carl and the Early Years of Psychoanalysis,* William Collins

Dethlefsen, Thorwald (1984) *The Challenge of Fate,* Coventure Ltd, Boston

Docherty, Nancy & West, Jacqueline

(2007) *The Matrix and Meaning of Character,* Routledge

Estes, Clarissa P. (1996) *Women Who Run With The Wolves,* Rider

Greene, Liz (1977) *Relating: An Astrological Guide to Living with Others on a Small Planet,* Red Wheel/Weiser, 2nd edition

(2008) *Astrology for Lovers,* Conari Press, illustrated edition

Guggenbuhl-Craig, Adolf
    (1995) *From the Wrong Side: A Perverse View of Psychology,* Spring Publications

    (2000) *The Emptied Soul: On the Nature of the Psychopath,* Spring Publications

    (2020) *Power in the Helping Professions,* Spring Publications

Hill, Gareth S.   (1992) *Masculine and Feminine,* Shambhala

Hillman, James   (1980) *Facing the Gods*, Chapter 1: On the necessity of Abnormal Psychology

Hillman, James & Shamdasani, Sonu
    (2013) *Lament of the Dead: Psychology After Jung's Red Book,* W.W. Norton & Co.

Hollis, James   (1994) *Under Saturn's Shadow,* Inner City Books

Hope, Eva   (1886) *Queens of Literature of the Victorian Era,* W.Scott, University of Michigan, digitized August 2010

Idemon, Richard   (1992) *Through the Looking Glass,* Samuel Weiser Inc.

Jaffe, Aniela   (1983) *C.G.Jung: Word and Image,* Princeton University Press, Bollingen Series

Johnson, Stephen M.   (1980) *The Symbiotic Character,* W.W. Norton & Company.

    (1985) *Characterological Transformation: The Hard Work Miracle,* W.W. Norton & Company.

    (1987) *Humanizing the Narcissistic Style,* W.W. Norton & Company.

    (1994) *Character Styles,* W.W. Norton & Company.

Johnson, Robert A.   (1974) *She,* Perennial Library, Harper & Row

    (1976) *He: Understanding Masculine Psychology,* Perennial Library, Harper & Row

    (1994) *Lying with the Heavenly Woman.* Harper, San Francisco

    (1983) *The Psychology of Romantic Love,* Arkana, Penguin Books Ltd.

Jung, C.G.	(1967) CW5 *Symbols of Transformation* A revision of *Psychology of the Unconscious,* 1912 Bollingen Series, Princeton University Press
	(1968) CW13 *Alchemical Studies,* Bollingen Series, Princeton University Press
	(1977) CW18 *The Symbolic Life,* Bollingen Series, Princeton University Press
Jung, Emma & von Franz, Marie-Louise	
	(1998) *The Grail Legend,* Princeton University Press; New Ed edition.
Kalsched, D.	(1996) *The Inner World of Trauma, Archetypal Defences of the Personal Spirit,* Routledge
	(2013) *Trauma and the Soul: A psycho-spiritual approach to human development and its interruption,* Routledge
King, Carole	(2012) *A Natural Woman,* Virago
Maslow, Abraham	(1962) *Toward a Psychology of Being,* Princeton, N.J.: D. Van Nostrand Company, Inc.
May, Rollo	(1991) *The Cry for Myth,* W.W. Norton & Company
Millman, Marcia	(2001) *The Seven Stories of Love: And How to Choose Your Happy Ending,* William Morrow
Millon, T. & Everly, G.S.	
	(1985) *Personality and its Disorders,* John Wiley & Sons
Moore, Thomas	(1990) *The Planets Within: The Astrological Psychology of Marsilio Ficino,* Lindisfarne Books, revised edition
	(1994) *Soul Mates,* Element Books Ltd
Paris, Ginette	(1986) *Pagan Meditations,* Spring Publications Inc.
Perrault, Charles	(1697) *Histoires ou Contes du temps passé,* Barbin, Paris
Perera, Sylvia Brinton	(1981) *Descent to the Goddess: A Way of Initiation for Women,* Inner City Books; first edition 1981
Picasso, Marina	(2001) *Picasso: My Grandfather,* New York: Riverhead.

Rudhyar, D. (1978) *The Pulse of Life*, Shambhala, Boulder & London, p.11

Sanford, John (1980) *The Invisible Partners*, Paulist Press

Street, Bill (2004) *The Astrology of Film: The Interface of Movies, Myth and Archetype*, iUniverse

Voytilla, Stuart (1999) *Myth and the Movies: Discovering the Mythic Structure of 50 Unforgettable Films*, Sheridan Books Inc.

Whitmont, Edward (1969) *The Symbolic Quest*, Princeton University Press; Expanded edition (1 Jan. 1979)

Woodman, Marion (1992) *Leaving My Father's House,* Shambhala Publications

Indexes

Main Index

A
addictions, 32, 98-99, 114-116
anxiety - chronic, 94
Aquarius, 6-8, 15-17, 73-89, 116, 121, 131
Aristophanes, 12
astrological axes
    ASC/DES, 18
    Aries/Libra, 6-7, 17, 109-110
    Cancer/Capricorn, 6-7, 28-45, 71, 128
    Gemini/Sagittarius, 6-7, 17, 58-62
    Leo/Aquarius, 6-7
    MC/IC, 18
    nodal axis, 19
    Taurus/Scorpio, 6-7, 17, 44-57, 84, 127-130
    Virgo/Pisces, 6-7, 92
attachment and bonding, 7, 29-30, 45

C
character armour, 30
character styles, 4, 6-8, 11, 15-16, 43, 128
    normal and neurotic, 8
    Oedipal, 111-113
    oral, 45-48
    masochistic, 91-93
    narcissistic, 75
    schizoid, 29
    symbiotic, 59
core fears
    abandonment, 10
    engulfment, 10

D
Dane Rudhyar, 13
Descartes, ix, 10
DSM-V, viii, 9
defence structures, 4-5, 62
defences – see personality traits
developmental goals, 8
    safety
    need
    self-agency
    self-esteem
    self determination
    self-expression
    survival, 30

E
ego, 1-5, 8, 10, 14-16, 22, 76-77, 84
ego ideal, 3-4, 77-78
equilibrium - axis of, 17, 110
Estes, Clarissa Pinkola, 51-52
exchange - axis of, 17, 44-57
exploration - axis of, 17, 58

F
Fairy Stories and Myths
    Abelard and Heloise, 66
    Artemis and Apollo, 110
    Beauty and the Beast, 52
    Bluebeard, 51
    Dionysus, vii, ix, 26
    grail myth, 80-84
    hero myths, 80
    Orion, 110
    Tantalus, 46

The Snow Queen, 87
Tristan and Isolde, 119
Ficino, Marsilio, 11, 139
films - theraputic function of, 25
Freud, vii-viii, 2, 8-9, 30,
  Oedipus complex, *112*
  psychosexual development, *110-112*
  vampire archetype, *101*

G

Gemini, 6-8, 17, 58-71, 108, 130
Gemini/Sagittarius axis, 58, 61-64, 71
grief and mourning, 36

H

health and wholeness - archetype, 98
heart - loss and recovery of, 79
host and parasite, 97
Hillman, James, viii

I

Idemon, Richard, 33
identity - axis of, 17, 73-89
identity confusion, 100
Incarnation - axis of, 17
individuation, 84

J

Jupiter, 17, 63, 67, 71, 84, 90-91, 106-108, 124, 126
Jung, Carl, 1, 8-10, 22, 53, 82-89, 135-139
Jung, Emma, 82-85

L

Leo/Aquarius axis, 6-7, 73-74

M

Mars, 17, 44, 54-57, 67, 88, 102-109, 114-116, 121
May, Rollo, 21
Mercury, 17, 41-42, 54, 58, 71, 88-90, 105, 108, 116, 121-126
Moon, 17, 28, 35, 39, 57, 71, 83, 87, 125
Myths - see Fairy Stories

N

Neptune, 17, 25, 54, 84, 90, 91, 102, 106, 127

O

Oedipus complex, 111-113
opposites - law of, 13

P

Personality disorders, 8-9
personality - provisional, 3-4
Personality traits - defensive adaptations
  anxiety – chronic, 95
  arrogance, 79
  cynicism, 63
  dependency/co-dependency, *92-94*
  deprivation, 45-48
  dissociation, 9, *111-113*
  enmeshment, 60
  entitlement, 45, 78
  fury, 77
  grandiosity, 74-76
  guilt, 18, 56, 60-66, 79, 87, 94-95, 124
  hypochondria, 77
  hysteria, *112-113*
  jealousy, 47, 111
  melancholy, 37
  moodiness, 33
  martyrdom, 96
  masochism, 92-96
  Messiah complex, 96
  narcissism, 74-79

obsession, 115
over-achievement, 76
panic, 60, 62, 63
paranoia, 48
passive aggression, 94-96, 107
possessiveness – extreme, 46
providing, 33, 46-49
rigidity, *115*
self-defeat, *93*
self-discipline, 115
self-sabotage, 77, 93-94
self-sacrifice, *95, 98*
rage, 47
rationalisation, 115
rescue, *93- 97*
rivalry, 65, 113
tension – chronic, 31
terror, 31
victimisation, 100
primal attachment and bonding, 7, 29
Plato, 11-12
Pluto, 17, 25, 43-44, 54-57, 84, 102-108, 116-127
postnatal depression, 30
Pisces, 6-8, 17, 67, 90-108, 132
Psychological syndromes
　Münchausen, *105*
　Münchausen by proxy, *106*
　Peter Pan, 38
　Stockholm, 104
psychopathology, vii, 9-10
psychosynthesis, 9

R

repetition compulsion, 5
resonance - law of, 14
Reich, Wilhelm, 3, 30

S

Sagittarius, 6-8, 17, 58, 59, 61-71, 102, 130

Saturn, 17, 28, 41- 42, 54, 57, 73, 77, 83, 102, 121, 125-127, 138
Self, 9
　false self, 3-4, 77-79, 114-115
　self-confidence, 10, 45, 59, 73, 74, 75
　self-esteem, 44-46, 65, 73, 75, 77, 90
　self-preservation, 32-34
　self-sufficiency, 30, 90
service - axis of, 17, 90-107
shadow, 5, 26, 53, 63, 83, 95-96, 109
Sun, 17, 19, 41-43, 54-57, 67, 71-73, 83, 88, 105, 108, 116, 121-127

T

transitional objects, 61

U

Uranus, 17, 41-43, 57, 71-73, 77, 87, 102, 121, 125-127

V

vampire archetype, 99-*100*
Venus, 17, 39, 43-44, 54-57, 71, 87-88, 102-109, 116, 121-126
Virgo, 6-8, 17, 90-108, 125, 132

W

wounded self, 6-8
　the abandoned child, 45
　the defeated child, 92
　the exploited child, 113
　the hated child, 29-32
　the rejected child, 113
　the unwanted child, 29-32, 45
　the owned/disowned child, 59-62
　the used child, 6-8, 74-75

Indexes

Actors, Artists and Musicians, Books and Films, Musicals, Writers and Playwrights

Actors

Abdul Salis, 130
Alan Rickman, 43, 133
Andrew Lincoln, 132
Anthony Hopkins, 57
Benedict Cumberbatch, 41
Bill Nighy, 128
Billy Bob Thornton, 131
Chiwetel Ejiofor, 132
Claudia Schiffer, 129
Clint Eastwood, 125
Colin Firth, 130
Demi Moore, 43
Dustin Hoffman, 43
Emma Thompson, 133
Glenn Close, 56, 71
Gregor Fisher, 128
Greta Garbo, 41
Hugh Grant, 131
Imelda Staunton, 124
Jack Black, 108
Jennifer Lawrence, 89
Jeremy Irons, 57
Joanna Page, 129
Jonathan Pryce, 71
Johnny Depp, 39
Jude Law, 108
Julia Roberts, 70, 86
Julianne Moore, 125
Julie Walters, 70
Juliet Stephenson, 43
Kate Winslet, 39, 71, 87, 108
Keira Knightley, 132
Kevin Costner, 43
Kris Marshall, 130
Laura Linney, 132
Leonardo de Caprio, 71, 87
Liam Neeson, 129
Lúcia Moniz, 130
Martin Freeman, 129
Martine McCutcheon, 131
Matt Damon, 108
Meryl Streep, 125
Michael Caine, 70
Michael Douglas, 56, 57
Olivia Olson, 129
Patrick Swayze, 43
Ralph Fiennes, 125
Richard Gere, 70, 86
Rodrigo Santoro, 132
Sarah Brightman, 108-109
Stephen Rea, 125
Thomas Sangster, 129
Tom Cruise, 88

Artists and Musicians

Andrew Lloyd Webber, 1*28*
Auguste Rodin, 71
Camille Claudel, 67
Carole King, *107*
Dante Gabriel Rossetti, *120*
Edward Burne-Jones, *121*
Eric Clapton, *124*
George Harrison, *124*
Jane Burden, *125*
Michael Jackson, 38
Pablo Picasso, 54-56

145

Tina Turner, *107*
Whitney Houston, 43, *107*
William Morris, *120*

Writers and Playwrights
Charles Dickens, 42
Clarissa Pinkola Estes, 51
D H Lawrence, 109, 125
Elizabeth Barrett Browning, 106
Emily Bronte, 103
Graham Greene, 125
Hans Christian Andersen, 87
Jane Austen, 86
John Cleese, 107
J.M. Barrie, 39
J.R.R. Tolkien, 41
Leo Tolstoy, 125
Lewis Carroll, 41
Marcel Proust, 41
Oscar Wilde, 107
Richard Curtis, 128
Rudyard Kipling, 41
Stephen King, 51

Books
A Natural Woman - Carole King, 107
Picasso My Grandfather - Marina Picasso, 55
Women who Run With The Wolves – Clarissa Pinkola Estes, 51

Books and Films
A Christmas Carol, 42
A Few Good Men, 88
A Perfect Murder, 57
Anna Karenina, 125
Basic Instinct, 57
Bridget Jones Trilogy, 86
Brief Encounter, 125
Crocodile Dundee, 70
Damage, 57
Dances with Wolves, 43
Dracula, 108
Educating Rita, 70
Falling Down, 57
Fatal Attraction, 50, 55
Finding Neverland, 39
Frozen and Frozen II, 87
Ghost, 43
Good Will Hunting, 43
Grand Hotel, 41
Harry Potter, 88, 124
Jack Reacher, 89
Jane Eyre, 86
Jerry Maguire, 89
Kafka, 57
Kramer vs Kramer, 43
Lady Chatterley's Lover, 125
Legally Blonde, 70
Lolita, 57
Love Actually, 129
Madame Bovary, 125
Madame Butterfly, 70
Midnight Cowboy, 43
Moulin Rouge, 70
My Fair Lady, 70
Notorious, 51
One Flew Over The Cuckoo's Nest, 124
Peter Pan, 37
Pretty Woman, 86
Pride and Prejudice, 86

Rainman, 43
Rebecca, 86
Revolutionary Road, 71
Romeo and Juliet, 42
Runaway Bride, 70
Sherlock Holmes, 41
Silence of the Lambs, 57
Tamara Drewe, 71
The Bodyguard, 43
The Bridges of Madison County, 125
The End of the Affair, 125
The Firm, 88
The Graduate, 43
The Holiday, 108
The Hunger Games, 88
The Imitation Game, 41
The King and I, 70
The Last of the Mohicans, 70
The Lord of the Rings, 88
The Phantom of the Opera, 108
The Shining, 51
The Sound of Music, 42
The Stepford Wives, 125
The Talented Mr Ripley, 108
The War of the Roses, 57
The Wife, 71
The Wizard of Oz, 88
Titanic, 70, 87
Tootsie, 43
Top Gun, 88
Truly Madly Deeply, 43
What's Love Got to Do With It, 107
Wuthering Heights, 101
You've Got Mail, 86

TV Series

Billions, 86
Downton Abbey, 42
Fawlty Towers, 107
Game of Thrones, 42
Succession, 86
The Crown, 42

Musicals

Miss Saigon, 70
The Phantom of the Opera, 10

About The Faculty of Astrological Studies

The Faculty of Astrological Studies was founded in London to raise the standard of astrological education. The Faculty remains at the forefront of the serious teaching of astrology, preserving the links to this ancient craft, embracing new developments and passing on this knowledge to students all over the world. Since its foundation in 1948, the Faculty has become known worldwide as a first class astrological school, and more than 10,000 students from over 90 countries have enrolled on its courses. Its Diploma is among the most highly valued and recognised international qualifications for the professional astrologer. Many of the worlds leading astrologers are or were Faculty Diploma holders, such as Dr Liz Greene, Charles Harvey, Julia Parker, Melanie Reinhart and Howard Sasportas.

The Faculty's team of dedicated tutors, all of whom are themselves Faculty Diploma holders, are devoted to teaching astrology to students all over the world, guiding them carefully from the very beginning of their astrological studies right through to professional qualification at Diploma level. The Faculty's courses are comprehensive and flexible, available online, by email and at classes in London. Some of the modules can also be studied at the Faculty's annual Oxford Summer School. Students can choose whichever method of learning suits them best, and alternate freely between them to suit their individual circumstances.

The Faculty's course material is unique, with a philosophical but practical approach to the art and craft of astrology, preserving its rich traditions and at the same time embracing and including modern psychological and post-psychological thinking. Course material is constantly updated, providing students with thorough, in-depth and comprehensive guidance, supported by their own personal tutor.

For further information visit: www.astrology.org.uk or write to: info@astrology.org.uk

About the Centre for Psychological Astrology

The Centre for Psychological Astrology was founded in 1983 by Dr Liz Greene and Howard Sasportas. Since its inception, the CPA has become world renowned for its unique and inspiring application of a variety of psychological approaches to astrology. The Centre continues to foster the cross-fertilisation of the fields of astrology and depth, humanistic and transpersonal psychology. Together with MISPA it hosts a unique webinar programme providing an original, informal and inspiring framework for both beginners and experienced astrologers.

Past CPA seminars are available as books and e-books through the CPA Press.

For further information about the current programme of seminars and webinars, to receive mailings and browse the CPA Press astrology books, visit: www.cpalondon.com or contact the Administrator, Juliet Sharman-Burke at: juliet@cpalondon.com

The **Online Introductory Certificate Course** with John Green provides a foundation in the basics of psychological astrology. Run as real time online tutorials, students can interact with the tutor and other students, ask questions and watch recorded sessions.

For further information, contact John at: webmaster@cpalondon.com

About the Mercury Internet School of Psychological Astrology

The Mercury Internet School of Psychological Astrology (MISPA) offers a 2 year Diploma Course, and students who have completed the CPA's Foundation Course, or similar, are eligible to enrol.

For further information visit: www.mercuryinternetschool.com or write to info@mercuryinternetschool.com

Clare Martin has an MA in Integrative Psychotherapy and has been a practising astrologer and teacher since 1990, working in London for the Faculty of Astrological Studies, of which she was President for nine years, and at the Centre for Psychological Astrology. Her personal approach to astrological interpretation is fundamentally Jungian, and evolved during a long period of studying with a variety of teachers in the western mystery traditions. Clare now lives in Dorset, where she continues her writing and consultancy work and is a tutor on the Mercury Internet School of Psychological Astrology.

Mapping the Psyche is a three volume introduction to psychological astrology, based on the transcriptions of a course Clare taught for many years at the Centre for Psychological Astrology. Their titles are as follows:

Volume 1: The Planets and the Signs of the Zodiac

Volume 2: Planetary Aspects and the Houses of the Horoscope

Volume 3: Kairos, the Astrology of Time

These books are an ideal entry point into astrology's symbolic language, and are recommended for anyone with a serious interest in discovering how astrology can enhance self-understanding and promote psychic integration.

Audience participation in these seminar style books ensures that psychological terms are fully explained and illustrated with personal examples. Clare draws from a variety of sources, including the perennial philosophy, alchemy and the kabbalah, demonstrating the inherently spiritual and magical dimensions of this approach to psychological astrology.

Clare's latest book, *Alchemy: The Soul of Astrology*, is proving a runaway hit. 25 years in the writing, this deceptively slim volume is innovative and ground-breaking. To give you more of an idea of the content, watch Clare's beautiful video and interview with Ana Isabel on the subject over on The Wessex Astrologer Youtube channel.

www.ingramcontent.com/pod-product-compliance
Lightning Source LLC
Chambersburg PA
CBHW060836190426
43197CB00040B/2656